Principles of Winning

Principles of Winning

Desmond D. Clark

PRINCIPLES OF WINNING

ISBN: 978-0-578-66992-2

CONTENTS

CHAPTER 1

WHY WRITE A BOOK ABOUT WINNING?

A quitter never wins—and a winner never quits.
—Napoleon Hill

Winning. It's one of the most frequently used words in the English language, yet it's also one of the most commonly ignored. Everyone likes to talk about winning. Coaches, politicians, business leaders, and parents all use the term to motivate people to perform, to achieve.

Vince Lombardi said winning isn't everything, but wanting to *is.* The hook of DJ Khaled's song goes, "All I do is win, win, win, no matter what." Some of us are like Tom Brady and the Patriots: we'll do anything to win—deflate balls, secretly film our opponents' practices, and who knows what else.

In this book, I'll share my version of what it means to win. While everything you read about here will be a product of my own life and my experiences as a former NFL player, a business professional, and a motivational speaker, I believe what I've learned can be learned and experienced by anyone.

I said that the word *winning* is frequently used and often ignored. I believe that if you asked one thousand people the simple question *would you like to be a winner,* you'd get 999 people who'd answer *yes,* and the only person who'd answer *no* would be someone who thought you said *sinner.* Everybody *wants* to win. Everybody is in love with the idea of winning. For most people, one of two things stands in the way of translating that desire into outcome: they lack the willingness to act, or they lack the knowledge of what to do. Some may lack both.

My goal in writing this book is to help you find the willingness to win and learn what it takes to become a winner. One thing I'm very aware of is that I can't share my experiences with anyone else. My experiences are unique to me and have been shaped by my own life and the people in it. What I can share is my story and the lessons I've drawn from it. I've learned from my father (you'll hear more about him in the next chapter), who has spent over twenty years in recovery; if I share those experiences with you, you'll take what you need and leave the rest behind.

People in general are drawn to what we call the "hero's journey." It's the story of overcoming adversity and rising to some level of greatness. Politicians are always trying to create that image for voters—whether it's true or not—because they know it will draw people to them. Professional athletes are often depicted as having traveled the hero's path because many have come from humble beginnings and our success makes people see us as aspirational figures. Our truth, my truth, is something different.

I never saw myself as making the hero's journey when I was growing up in Lakeland, Florida, and dealing with a father who was struggling with addiction and a mother who was spreading herself so thin to support us that there was barely anything left of her at the end of the day. My goal was just to try to get through each day and get to the next one. If I made the hero's journey, it's not because I set out that way.

What I did do, however, was set out to improve myself and to win. I was determined and motivated from a very early age. I knew that the life I had wasn't the life I wanted. Both my older brothers would say about me that "Desmond always had a plan. Desmond was organized." I knew if I was going to escape the life I had in Lakeland that nobody was going to rescue me. I was going to have to rescue myself.

When I was in middle school, there was a guard on the basketball team who was a far superior player. I was athletic, but I was nowhere near as good as he was at shooting hoops. I set myself the goal of becoming a guard on the team and becoming even better than he was. My mother and brothers would hear me outside practicing my dribbling well after dark each night, to the point where they would bring me in because they couldn't stand the noise. I was torturing them, but I was working on my game. I had a plan.

I was working at winning, and that work paid off. I became the basketball player I wanted to be; my teammates could judge whether or not I surpassed the young man I was chasing. What I know for sure is that I got to where I had set my sights. On a personal level, I won.

What I was learning, without realizing it at the time, was that in making the conscious commitment to become the best guard on the basketball team, and putting forth the effort to make it happen, I was simply unlocking what was already inside of me. I could have been the best guard earlier if I had started sooner, and I would have never been the best guard if I hadn't picked up the ball at all. The ability to win was inside me. I just had to set it loose.

During the incredible journey that has been my life, I've been an active participant in it and I've taken mental notes. Those mental notes are what makes it possible for me to write this book. They are what allow me to address groups of business professionals and amateur athletes and all sorts of people in between. No matter who I address, even though I customize my message toward the age group or the organization I'm speaking to, the fundamental truth I share is always the same: everyone has it in them to be a winner. If you can find a way to use what's already in you, you'll do well. My goal in writing this book is to help you find that something that's already inside you. I'm not suggesting that everybody needs my help to win, but I do believe that everybody needs *somebody's* help to win.

During my life, I've met people who made a real difference in getting me to where I am now, a place from which I plan to continue to ascend, shift, and win. I'll share bits and pieces of their thoughts and stories, where it's appropriate, to help make a point. They include the usual suspects that you might expect in anyone's life and those you would guess were involved in any athlete's life. My mother and father led the way, although throughout my early life my mother was my inspiration for the kind of person I wanted to be, while my father, through his active addiction, was teaching me the opposite lesson.

My older brothers were also inspirational. We shared the belief that the kind of story we are all writing by living today is not a story we were meant to be around to write. If you were a group of boys coming up in a somewhat fragmented, black family in the drug-torn parts of Lakeland, the odds were that at least one of you was going to end up in jail, in an institution, or dead. We all made it, and we did so in large part because we had each other. None of us were perfect, but each of us was there for the others.

I had several coaches and teammates along the way who also helped shape my life. Not all the coaches gave me a lot of playing time, and some of my teammates were my direct position competitors. In those instances, what I learned is that even with elements of built-in friction, people are still capable of helping others and lifting them up. I needed Coach Mike Martz (who didn't play me much) and tight end Shannon Sharpe to help teach me how to win just as much as I needed the friendlier mentors.

I see my role in writing this book as one that's similar to the role those people and others played in my life. I'm trying to share a part of me that might help teach you how to win. I have a friend who told me that when he was seventeen, he somewhat inexplicably read a book on current events and economics. That chance reading set the course for his life and today he is successful in the world of political writing. For somebody reading this book, I can only hope it has that kind of effect on your life.

Everybody likes a list. I could just write a couple hundred pages about winning and do it in an open, free-flowing way that tells stories and draws on lessons. Unfortunately, that makes it tough for the reader to keep it all straight. I don't want you to spend the effort reading this book and at the end of it ask yourself, "Now, what was Desmond saying again?"

To that end, after telling you a little bit about my personal history (Chapters 2 and 3), I've divided the book into what I've identified as the five key steps to winning in sports, winning in school, winning in business, and just plain winning in life. They are:

- Protecting your name and your word (Chapter 4)
- The power of relationships (Chapter 5)
- Maintaining a commitment to excellence (Chapter 6)
- Being self-motivated (Chapter 7)
- Having passion and purpose (Chapter 8)

While you might look at those five steps and think that you've seen them before, I can promise you that you haven't. I say that because even if you've been discussing those five steps every day for the past year, what you haven't done is to learn about them from my perspective. I intend to share with you how I actively experience each of the five steps and through that process, I hope to leave you with useful pieces that you can use as part of your own approach to winning.

In addition to the five steps, I also want to help fill your toolbox with the things you'll need to win. Imagine that each of the five steps above are ones you want to take yourself. It's easier to climb if you have the right equipment. Here are some of the concepts I keep in mind as I take my daily steps toward winning: focus, discipline, self-awareness, introspection, authenticity, resiliency, and staying real. I've also developed the discipline of asking myself some tough questions with each experience: What did I learn? What did I do wrong? How can I change in the future? How can this help me start winning in this area? It's only through the process of applying critical thought to actual experiences that you can grow and improve in your life.

If you're wondering, before you get too much further along, whether or not you should continue reading this book, or maybe recommend it to a friend to read at the same time so you can discuss, ask yourself if you fall into one of the following categories:

- Do you feel like you want to reach your peak but right now you're stuck or, worse, complacent?
- Are you always looking for new ideas and approaches to add to your repertoire?
- Are you already winning in life but feel you want to keep winning and might benefit from some new tactics to assist in that effort?

I hope that if you, or someone you know, falls into one of these categories, you will benefit from continuing to read. I also hope that reading this book will encourage you to open up and share your story. Too often people think that if they aren't a celebrity, nobody would want to hear what they have to share. They ask, "Why would anyone care?" I can tell you that everybody has a story worth sharing because everybody has somebody who can relate.

We spend a lot of time in our own heads. We think we're alone. We aren't. One of the many things I've learned from my father's recovery is that anyone can share something, no matter how seemingly insignificant, that can have a life-changing impact on someone else. I'm being up front in letting you know that I want to try to help change and improve your life by sharing my approach to winning. What I want you to know is that you can change and improve lives, too!

I hear some of you saying, "But, Desmond, I'm too old to start winning. The time for me to win has passed. Now it's up to my kids and grandkids." While I can appreciate how you might have that feeling, my response is that if you have a vision beyond where you are at the moment, it's never too late to move toward that vision. All of us are eventually going to draw a last breath. While we wait for that moment, it makes no sense to waste all the breaths we have before that final one. We all know the story of Colonel Sanders and how success came to him late in life. Your story doesn't need to be his story. It just needs to be the one that you want to write.

An inspirational moment can come at any time and at any age. I remember being this poor kid in Lakeland, Florida who, as part of our school's basketball team, went to New York City during my junior year for basketball camp. My family was so poor that my best friend's family pitched in to get me a pair of new sneakers before I left. While in New York, we had a chance to stand at the top of the World Trade Center. The view was beyond anything I could have imagined. I had gone, in a moment's time, from peeking around a street corner to see if there was danger, to looking at what appeared to be the entire world all at once.

In that moment I thought to myself that I wasn't just some dirty kid from Florida. I was going to win. I was going to get out. I was going to make it. I happened to have been seventeen at the time. I could just as easily have been fifty-seven. I could have been Colonel Sanders. But I wasn't. I was Desmond Clark and I had already started living my story. From that moment on though, I started taking notes. I took them because I knew I was going to win.

Philosophically speaking, everything suggested by someone has an opposite. The opposite of winning is, of course, losing. Sometimes, losing is easy to identify. In an athletic competition, when the game ends somebody has more points than another (or less in golf) and the one on the wrong end of the count can be said to have lost. In an election, once the votes are counted, the loser is clearly identified. In athletics and elections, losers are clear because you determine them after the fact. In life, defining when losing begins or ends isn't quite so clear.

There's a mindset around losing that I believe comes from a person thinking they just don't have what it takes to get the job done on their own. They think negative thoughts and we know that those negative thoughts can ultimately impact how your brain works. Your brain becomes trained to lose. You need to be training your brain to win.

People also lose because they focus on their limitations. This is the metaphorical equivalent of letting yourself freeze to death out in the cold because you don't have a match to start a fire. A limitation, sure, but rubbing sticks together would have saved your life. Some limitations we face are permanent, while others are temporary. Regardless of the nature of the limitation, if you want to win you have to force yourself to find a way to work around it and not just accept losing.

Another reason we lose is surrounding ourselves with the wrong people. For example, where I grew up, drugs and crime were a part of daily life. It was so bad that people didn't just tolerate that kind of life in others, they actually expected that kind of life for other people. I know so many people who didn't make it out of our neighborhood because of the people they surrounded themselves with—they almost never had a chance. My brothers and I used athletics as a way to surround ourselves with better people who could take turns lifting us up, not dragging us down.

A certain way to lose instead of win is to have an attitude of "blame another first" before looking at yourself. This is easier to use in the world of business than it is in athletics. In sports, we have video to let us go back and replay what really happened: "Desmond, you missed the block, that's why I went down." The tape shows otherwise. In real life, we don't usually have tapes to replay. It's easier to blame others and get away with it.

However, we can only get away with it in the eyes of others. We are the ones who *really* matter. There's an old expression that says, "You're only fooling yourself." In the blame game, it's actually the opposite. You might fool other people, but deep down you know that you're responsible for your own loss. Taking personal responsibility and ownership are keys to winning and not losing.

I recently was impacted by listening to a motivational expert make the statement that when winners are presented with data that shows they are losing, they adjust their behavior and find a way to win. When losers are presented with the same data, they turn to excuses and blame circumstances or others.

Someone told me a story of a person who was fired by one of the big, international consulting companies. When she was let go, the manager asked her if she wanted to know why it didn't work out.

"Of course, I'd love to know," she said.

"Because you just aren't linear enough. We are a very linear company and you just don't think in a linear fashion."

While that may have gotten somebody fired from a stodgy Brooks Brothers environment, that's exactly the kind of person who has the best shot at winning in life. The reason? We don't live in a linear world.

My life timeline, in terms of success and failure, looks more like an EKG chart than it does a straight line. I've bounced back and forth between success and failure. My periods of success have sometimes appeared accelerated while periods of adversity have seemed elongated in comparison. Adversity has raised its head many times. I've been divorced. I've been let go from teams when I had no expectation it was coming. I've been conned out of significant money by people I trusted. I've lost. This is life on life's terms, not yours.

As that great philosopher Rocky Balboa, taught us:

> Let me tell you something you already know. The world ain't all sunshine and rainbows. It's a very mean and nasty place and I don't care how tough you are, it will beat you to your knees and keep you there permanently if you let it. You, me, or nobody is gonna hit as hard as life. But it ain't about how hard you hit. It's about how hard you can get hit and keep moving forward. How much you can take and keep moving forward. That's how winning is done!

Perhaps that quote from a fictional character could have been this whole first chapter: be prepared for setbacks. Be prepared for them when you least expect them. Know that it might take longer to recover something than it took to get it in the first place.

When I went through my divorce and lost nearly everything that mattered to me, I told my brother, "It's OK. I'm going to get everything back in one year. All I need is 365 days." He thought I was crazy, and my timeline was a bit off, but I made it. I followed my five steps and worked relentlessly. I practiced what I'm about to preach to you. It got me through, and I hope what I share can help do the same for you.

When you have finished this book, I hope that I'll have helped you to be able to, and be willing to, take a few of the steps I've created, the steps that have worked so well for me, and implement them in your life. It would be the most humbling experience to meet you on the street (yes, you can approach me on the street) and have you say, "Desmond, that point you made in your book really made the difference for me." That's why I'm writing this—so you can get the key piece that can make the difference between winning and losing.

I once heard a news analyst tell listeners, "I read the newspaper every day so you don't have to." When you write a book about life lessons that's another main objective. You would love to have people not have to learn things the hard way, the way you learned them. Every parent has the same wish for their child: that their sins will be their own (I'll have you relate to that in the next chapter). Hopefully, this book will help you not commit some of the "sins" of my past.

If you've decided that maybe this book isn't for you (and you're going to use it to balance that wobbly couch in your family room), please take this away as a gift from me: *Everything you need to be a winner truly is inside of you. If this book isn't the key to help you to unlock it, that's OK. Different keys open different doors. Find your key and unlock the winner that stands ready to emerge.*

Let's get started. Before you understand my steps to winning, you need to understand a little bit more about my life story. Before you can understand that, you need to understand my father's story. For better and for worse, he's the person from who I've learned the most. He's the man who taught me what it takes to win.

CHAPTER 2

BY THE SINS AND VIRTUES OF MY FATHER

> Fathers, do not embitter your children, or they will become discouraged.
>
> —Colossians 3:21

Fort De Soto Beach is part of Fort De Soto Park located in Pinellas County, Florida. The entire park consists of five connected islands (keys) and just over a thousand acres. Located on the gulf side of the state near Clearwater and St. Petersburg, the beaches are regularly voted among the top in the US. The area is a popular attraction for tourists, snowbirds, and locals.

For me, that beach is more than nice place to take my family on vacation. For me, it provides bookends for a chapter in my life that took place many years ago, spanning just over a decade, and which helped make me the man I am today. That beach was the setting for two key moments in what was the intersection between my boyhood and my father's journey through drug addiction.

My father, Paul Clark, was born in 1957 in Fort Lauderdale. His mother and father made a relatively quick, but not quite complete, exit from his life and he was left to be raised by his grandparents in Lakeland, a city forty miles east of Tampa. While his mother moved north to New York State, his father remained in the area and was an in-and-out presence in his life.

My father's two primary male role models were his grandfather and his uncle, both of whom were contracted crop-picking workers. He tells me that his grandfather was an alcoholic and when he wasn't drinking, he was a very mean "dry drunk," someone who exhibits the bad behavior of an alcoholic minus having the actual alcohol in their system. When my father was thirteen, his grandfather died, leaving just him and his grandmother at home to make a go of it.

They were poor and they were black: my father was very aware of both those circumstances. He recalls being a young boy and having white kids tease him about his very dark skin color. Once when he got home, his grandfather caught him in the bathtub scrubbing furiously. When asked what he was doing, my father replied, "Trying to wash the black off."

The black didn't come off and neither did the stains of poverty. His grandma worked a job on the 3-11 shift, so once he got home from school, he was kind of on his own. In Lakeland at that time, being black and being on your own often meant being on the streets. Those streets were nothing more than a drug-addicted life waiting to happen.

My father took to those streets. He began experimenting with drugs and alcohol. At the same time he was learning the streets, he was also showing signs of the struggle that would live within him for years: the struggle between wanting to do good while just wanting to be free to use. He started working at his first job, at a dollar store, when he was only eleven years old; later he worked at a local TV shop cleaning up. Until his grandfather died, my dad would split his earnings with him. After his passing, he would contribute to help his grandmother keep the house afloat. He also did migrant crop work. Maneuvering a loader in the orange grove before he was even legally old enough to drive, he earned the nickname Fruit Hog because he could gather so much so fast.

As a teenager, my father still had a chance. He was torn between the tempting life of drugs and the responsible life of self-sacrifice and self-determination. While he had no particular dreams for his future, save for maybe being a racecar driver with his '71 Chevy Nova, he also didn't want to end up on the streets. He managed to avoid that fate, for a while.

When he was an older teenager, he met a beautiful young girl named Rena, my mother. Rena already had a son, Ralph, from a previous relationship and my father took him in and treated him as if he were his own. Together they had two sons, my older brother Paul Jr. and me. All of this took place before they were married. They made it official in 1979, when the preacher came to our house for a simple ceremony. If only the promises made on that day, before God and his witnesses, had held. Who knows what life might have been like? Then again, the life I had made me the man I am today. I'm not complaining, just pondering.

My dad has shared with me that when he became a father, his goal was to not have his children live the kind of life he had been forced to live. He wanted to make sure he was there for us so that we never felt alone or neglected. In our very early years, it was that thought that motivated him, and it was that thought that let us enjoy what were our very best days as a family.

When I was born, our family lived in a part of Lakeland known to the locals as Black Bottom. The area is bounded by West 10th Street, Amos Avenue, West Crawford Street, and Martin Luther King Jr. Avenue. Your guess as to why part of its name is "Black" is likely incorrect—that part refers to the neighborhood's absence of streetlights in the past. The other part of the name "Bottom," well, you guessed that part right. Black Bottom was low on income and low on hope but high on crime and everyone was high on drugs. That's where we started. My dad wouldn't have it. He worked his way to becoming a professional tile installer and he got us out.

We had some really good times. Our apartment was nice and roomy, so much so that we were the place that family and friends would come for barbeques. That was something my parents enjoyed hosting. My dad was larger than life to me. I can remember being young and running at him full speed down our hallway and just jumping on him as hard as I could. It never occurred to me I might hurt him. He was my dad. He couldn't be hurt. He was indestructible. He was my hero.

We wanted for nothing. We weren't rich but it sure didn't feel like we were poor. We had the new Atari game system, go-carts, a motorcycle, and even a pool table that was the focal point when family would come over for those barbeques.

There was a moment during those glory days when I got glimpse of what was on our family's horizon. I was just a little too young, and my deductive powers were too underdeveloped for me to fully grasp it. My father was in our bathroom and hadn't locked the door. I walked in and surprised him while he was snorting cocaine. He had taken the leaf from the dining room table and laid it across our bathtub in order to place his "lines" on it. When he saw me, he hurriedly tried to cover it up and offered some explanation I can no longer recall.

I knew something was wrong, but I just didn't understand what.

Little did I know, it would only be a few years later that my brother and I would be lighting his crack cocaine pipe for him because shotgun pellets had taken his eyesight.

I have a memory, maybe from around age seven, of the whole family taking a spontaneous trip to Fort De Soto Beach. Dad had just gotten home from the hospital and the very next day decided we should have a family outing. I remember being excited to go and I also remember thinking it was pretty cool that my dad had just gotten home from the hospital, hand all wrapped in bandages, and he was taking us out for a day of fun. What a great dad. My hero.

What I didn't realize is that my dad's hand was wrapped in bandages because he had been shot. It seems that he had been out drinking and drugging with a local dude name Spiderman (I suspect this "Spiderman" was *not* a superhero). They were shooting craps when an argument started, and Spiderman pulled a gun. He fired a shot that went through my father's hand and into his side. My dad was taken to the hospital. My mother told us he was there but not what had happened. When he came home and decided we were going to the beach, my brothers and I figured there must not be anything to worry about.

So, off we went to Fort De Soto. Little did I know that was the beginning of the end of our semi-idyllic family life.

It took my dad a bit of time to develop into the full-blown drug addict he would eventually become. His experiments with drugs and alcohol had started back in high school, but he was able to keep it under control. His use was recreational in the way that term exists in the world of Black Bottom Lakeland. It's true that he managed to acquire a skill, maintain steady employment, and provide for his family. It's also true that he was living right on the edge the entire time.

Eventually, my father got envious of his uncle who was a known drug dealer. His uncle always seemed to have money. Imagine what my dad could do if he had money? Dad started selling drugs down on Roselle Street, a virtual mini mart in the Lakeland drug world. While Al Pacino taught us in 1983's *Scarface* to "not get high on your own supply," my dad apparently didn't see that movie. He became his own best customer—such a good customer, in fact, that he had a hard time keeping his work orders straight. That kind of bad business practice eventually got him shot a second time, after he had botched a client's drug package. This time he was shot in both legs, the other hand, and his groin.

It's said that people suffering from addiction need to hit bottom before they can turn their lives around. Well, my dad bounced. That second shooting incident wasn't enough to get him to get clean, and neither was the third. In that third incident, he was again drugging with someone, there was the usual altercation, and this time his adversary produced a shotgun. All my father says he remembers is seeing the pellets coming toward him. It was the last thing he would ever see: that shotgun blast cost him his eyesight.

It's hard to describe the impact of knowing your father can no longer see because of a shotgun blast to the face. I remember walking around my house with a towel over my eyes so I could try to experience what he must have been experiencing. Of course, a temporary towel blinder is not the equivalent of facing permanent blindness. I could never truly get it. Nor could I understand the rest of what he was experiencing.

As was the case with so many cocaine users in the late 1970s and early 1980s, my father's habit spiraled out of control when he transitioned from inhaling to smoking cocaine. Crack cocaine remains one of the most instantly addictive of all illegal drugs. Once my father started down that path in about 1984, he never had a chance. So deep was his addiction that once he lost his sight, he would have my brother or me light up for him. Neither one of us ever told the other we were doing it, for fear that they would be mad at the other for enabling Dad. We only discovered it a few years later by sharing Dad's drug war stories.

Dad's addiction ultimately led to the end of his marriage with my mom. She had taken all she could. Mom did everything in her power to protect us from the ravages of dad's demons but ultimately it was just too much. By the time I finished third grade, my dad was out of our home. The home that had once held so much so love and joy was now just a memory-filled empty place we couldn't afford. We had to move.

It was back to Black Bottom.

It was July 4, 1997. Not only was it the nation's birthday, but also my father's fortieth birthday. He had taken us to Fort De Soto Beach and was sitting by the gulf smoking a cigarette and having a drink. At least he wasn't smoking crack. He had already managed to give that up by that point. Dad had finally gotten tired of always being broke. He felt guilty for selling our things to pay for drugs. He was sick of having to bum money from family members and the few friends he had left. The day came where he smoked his last bit of coke, walked himself (remember he was blind) to the Lakeland Regional Medical Center, and checked himself into rehab.

He hasn't done drugs since.

Sitting on the beach that day with his cigarette and his drink, he took one last long drag. He looked at the cigarette, put it out in the sand, and said, "This is the last cigarette I'm gonna smoke." A few minutes later, he took the final sip from his drink, set down the empty, and said, "That's the last drink I'm gonna take."

Those were the last cigarette and last drink my father ever had. I witnessed that moment. No drama. No long speech. No music playing in the background. Just a simple "that's it." And it was.

That moment at Fort De Soto marked both an end and a new beginning. The interesting part is that even though I had lost parts of my dad during his twelve-year run with addiction, he never stopped being my dad. And I never stopped learning from him. Even deep in his addiction to crack cocaine, he was still teaching his son lessons.

And there were many.

This is a book about winning. More specifically, it's a book about a path to winning that I've developed and followed over the course of my life. That means it's the product of my life's work up until this point. And it means that every experience I've had has been incorporated, consciously or subconsciously. I'm certain that the experience of growing up with a father suffering from addiction has had the greatest overall impact on me and how I've lived my life since.

It was difficult to navigate those years. At my young age, and with the severity of my father's problems, I was not well equipped to handle the fallout. It's not like you can go to the library and check out a book titled "*How to Deal with Dad Who Gets Shot Three Times—and Still Keeps Using!*" That book wasn't on the shelves then, and I doubt if it's even on an internet blog today. My mother, my brothers, and I were making it up as we went along and holding on to each other. We were trying to survive. To borrow a phrase from the recovery world, we were just living one day at a time.

It would be too easy to tell you that the key to winning is to just look at what my father did in his life and "do the opposite." Obviously, crack cocaine and winning don't go well together. The kind of "scoring" a crack addict tries to achieve isn't the kind of scoring we associate with winning. That said, discounting my father's life and trivializing it by essentially saying "don't do drugs and you can win," is not only a cliché, but also does a disservice to who he was and is as a person and what he taught me.

My father is a good man who lived a significant part of his life badly. That means his impact on my life is complicated and layered. Some of the lessons I learned about winning were because of him, some were despite him, and some were directly from him. I think it's too easy for us to look at a person in our lives who has made serious mistakes or done something that wasn't right and then completely discount their value as a human being. That's tragic.

People should be evaluated based on the sum total of their life as they've lived it. That's what I've tried to do with my dad. I'll share some of the things I learned through my youthful journey with him before, during, and after his active addiction. Those experiences have everything to do with my approach to winning.

A primary lesson from my father's addiction actually was taught to me by my mother. Throughout my dad's dark journey, despite the way he betrayed his wife and his sons, my mother refused to trash talk him to us. Her messages, customized to every disappointing event, can be summarized by the line, "He's your father. Love him and respect him."

My mother refused to destroy his name with us. That meant that when he finally got clean from drugs my senior year of high school, I didn't have to get ready to accept him back into my life because he was already there. He had just been standing right outside the door, welcome to walk in anytime he was ready. My mother protected his name and by doing so helped to teach me the value of protecting a name. That became part of my formula for winning.

Years later, I also thought back to that moment in the bathroom, when I surprised my dad while he was doing lines of coke. His clumsy attempt to cover up what he was doing was his own failed way of trying to protect his name in front of his son. I've taken this lesson to heart with my own children. While I'm committed to being honest with them at all times, I'm just as committed to making sure that, since I'm honest, I don't do things that will make them feel ashamed once they learn about them.

Another key lesson was the importance of maintaining relationships. While my dad was using drugs, perhaps in part *because* he was using drugs, he was completely unfiltered and non-judgmental in his conversations. My brothers and I could talk to him about absolutely anything. And we did! Even though we were not getting a clear-headed father, we were getting at least a part of a father, and a sometimes entertaining one at that. His openness, genuine or otherwise, left a door open for us to maintain a relationship. It taught me how important it was not to let go of anyone.

My mother played a key role in driving home the power of relationships, as well. One of her favorite expressions was to say to my brothers and me, "As long as we have us, we have enough." Given our circumstances, that wasn't always the easiest thing to remember or to believe. It turned out, however, that she was right. It's a lesson I teach to my children today.

Going back to that first moment when I needed to light my dad's pipe for him because of his lost eyesight, that was perhaps the most negative teachable moment I remember experiencing. By that, I mean I knew that I never wanted to be like the man I was seeing before me. The feelings were strong. I thought, *you're a bum and I'll never let myself be like you.* That created a sense of self-motivation in me.

In sales they teach you that trying to motivate a customer to buy by talking negatively about a competitor or about what they are currently using is a tactic certain to fail. While people might like to complain for the purpose of letting off steam, getting them in a negative frame of mind doesn't usually translate into getting them to write a check.

It's the same with making positive changes in your attitude and life. Like the word says, positive change requires some form of positive motivation. Not wanting to become what my father was set a hard deck below which I would not let myself fall. If I wanted to win, I still needed something aspirational that I wanted to reach, something positive.

I found positive motivation in the eyes of my mother. In choosing my father as a partner, what seemed to be a good choice at the time turned out to be a very disappointing one. My father had let her down. She worked so hard and set such a good example that she just didn't deserve that. At the same moment, I was deciding not to become my father, I was also deciding that I was going to live a life that made my mother proud. This was my aspiration. That was a form of self-motivation that could keep me moving in a positive, forward-looking direction.

When my father sat on Fort De Soto Beach and put out that cigarette and put down that drink, it taught me something about passion and purpose. The same lesson had shown up earlier in his blind man's walk to the rehab center. We've all known addicts who never make it. They wind up in jail, in an institution, or dead. My father had actually been in two of the three and had come awfully close to the third. He had only passed through those places. He didn't end up there. That accomplishment required a deep sense of purpose to enable him to pull himself through and keep moving forward. I witnessed that sense of purpose that day on the beach in its simplest, stripped-down form. At least he made it look simple.

The truth is that what my father accomplished in that moment was only to commence what has become an ongoing, one day at a time accomplishment ever since. Sobriety and a clean lifestyle can be maintained only with relentless personal vigilance. An addict's work is never done. They are always just one hit away from undoing everything they have accomplished. They need to have a passion for sobriety and act with purpose in order to maintain that passion. If my father had never traveled through the darkness of addiction, I never would have been able to watch the determination he used to move past it.

I mentioned in the previous chapter that in order to win, you need certain tools to help you along the way. One of those tools is resiliency and another is self-awareness or introspection. My father went through a period in his life that would have killed most men and would have made cynics out of the few that survived. My dad, however, is no cynic. He has come through this with a positive attitude not only about the future, but also about the past.

"It wasn't the drugs that got me, it was my attitude. I had a temper and it got the best of me. I never gave anyone a chance." This is my dad's honest take on himself and why he made the mistakes he made. He doesn't portray himself as a victim, but rather as a volunteer. He signed up for the life he lived. He is accountable. He also says, "I've been a winner all my life. Even in the bad times." Dad realizes that everything he ever needed to win has always been inside him. He may have set it aside for a while but it was still there.

This is the sign of a resilient man. These are the signs of an introspective and self-aware man who has taken his own fearless and searching moral inventory and decided he is ok. If he can have his perspective today then I know that I have no excuses in life if I fail to achieve. I also know I can't lie to myself. I need to be constantly looking inside and keeping track of who I am and where I am. I don't want to get off track. If I do, I'm going to bounce back. I'm not going to blame anybody else. I'm just going to do what I need to do. I learned that from my dad. I learned it the hard way.

When I got to the NFL, surrounded by all the glitz and glamour that is America's *real* pastime, my father once asked me, "Son, do I embarrass you?" I almost got mad at him for asking, and I told him in some very clear language that of course he didn't embarrass me. He was and is my dad. I'm proud of him. I love having him around and having him in my life. I never thought twice about it.

But he did. Imagine what my father lived through and the awareness he has of the mistakes he made and the hurt that he caused. That is a burden that no matter how great his spirit, no matter his own commitment to winning, that he will always carry. When he asked me years after he had gotten clean and sober if he was an embarrassment, it really wasn't about that moment. It was about the baggage from all the moments before, years ago, when my brothers and I were forced to go through boyhood without him being truly present.

But we never quit. He never quit. We learned lessons about the importance of protecting your name and how it matters to keep your word and how it hurts when you don't. We became self-motivated. Nobody was going to get anything done for us. We had to rely on ourselves. That being said we did have each other and those relationships, though sometimes tenuous, held together and held us together. We developed a purpose for our lives and pursued it with passion.

While it might not have looked like it, we were pursuing excellence. We were all striving to be the very best we could be. The bar of excellence may have seemed quite low at first, but as it kept rising, we kept climbing. All of us. My dad, too.

We are still climbing—my dad, my brothers, and me. And now our children and families are climbing too. All of us turned out well, despite almost impossible odds. All of us, for better or worse, are a product of my father's addiction and his many years of triumphs and tragedies in his fight. His story made our story.

Today, for all of us, it's a story of winning.

CHAPTER 3

Growing Up Physically, Spiritually, and Not at All Easily

That which does not kill us makes us stronger.
—Friedrich Nietzsche

Winning is a skill, not a talent. This means it can be, has to be, learned. I wasn't born to be a winner and neither is anyone else. Some people are born into a set of circumstances that might make the path to learning to win seem easier, but that doesn't mean they don't have to put in the time to study and practice. It just means that their personal "gym" or their "classroom" might be better equipped with tools to assist them in their efforts.

The set of circumstances I was born into certainly didn't make my path to learning to win easier to navigate. I've shared the story of my father's journey through addiction and the poverty and uncertainty it created for my mother, my siblings, and me. But I also had one extraordinary advantage that others with more financial and familial stability might not have. I had a mother who was relentless in her efforts to be there for us and support us in every aspect of our lives. Her tireless commitment to excellence as a parent certainly gave me some sort of early childhood education on winning in life.

It goes without saying that part of the learning process is trial and error—*error* being an antiseptic word for losing. I lost plenty along the way. Since I'm an athlete, people assume that when I say *lost,* I'm referring to losing games. There were plenty of those occasions but what I mean by losing isn't about final scores. It's about making decisions that turn out to be wrong; those decisions are losses. One of the great things I've learned about free will is that if you choose well, you live well. If you choose poorly or if you lose, you get to choose again.

With the idea in mind that winning is a skill and that our successes and failures along the way are a major part of how we learn, allow me to share some of the experiences from my formative years, the sum total of which have contributed to making me the man I am today and have provided me with the spiritual calling to write this book and, hopefully, help you learn how to win in life without having to suffer some of my losses.

While my message to you isn't about winning as an athlete, the fact is that I was an athlete and it was through my participation in sports that I learned many of my lessons about winning. I'm no different than the corporate CEO who shares the life lessons they acquired through their business experience. The danger in being an athlete and writing a book about winning is that everything can start to sound like a sports metaphor. I ask that you not get lost in the sports context. The stories and the experiences I'll share from my athletic career are real and I believe they are transferable.

My athletic voyage started at the age of six or seven playing midget football under Coach Jerry Odom. I was fortunate to have him as my first coach because what I remember about him primarily is how he made playing football fun. At such a young age we aren't necessarily in the mindset to start learning life lessons, but what we do know instinctively is whether or not we like something. Who knows how my life would have turned out if Coach Odom had made me hate the experience of playing football? We respond differently as people to the sensations of pleasure and pain. He made football pleasurable and it made me want more of it.

A quick side note to anyone who gets involved in coaching their very young child's youth sports activity: the process can seem chaotic and while it feels more like herding cats than it does teaching anything, please remember that you're teaching something very important just by the quality of the experience you create and the energy you bring to every practice. Coach Odom did that for me and you can do it for your kids and their teammates.

The first person to have a significant and lasting impact on me through my later elementary school years was football coach Raymond Gunder. Coach Gunder had coached my older brother and he could see the talent in me and helped me to see it in myself. He was so influential in my life that while I was playing for him at what we called the junior varsity (JV) level, he switched teams and I switched with him. (In Lakeland, most participation in the sports leagues was outside of the school system until you reached either middle school or high school.) He and I left the Lakeland Lumberjacks and went to the Lakeland Patriots. In that place and time, it would have been the equivalent of turning down a contract extension with the

Chicago Bears and signing as a free agent with the Green Bay Packers. It was an act of treason. Coach Gunder made committing that act of treason worth it.

Coach Gunder was the adult male I needed in my life. He was looked at by parents in the area as a sort of inspirational figure to whom their children could be influenced. Looking back, it's likely that some of the parents themselves looked up to him. I remember one day when my brother was not home when he was supposed to be and my mother was fit-to-be-tied. There was no question that he was going to get the sternest of her punishments when he got home. When he finally walked in the door and said he'd been with Coach Gunder, Mom's anger instantly turned into relief and all was forgiven. She knew he was benefiting from the time.

There are all sorts of positive words and phrases that come to my mind when I think about my experience with Coach Gunder. He was a good role model. He showed me what success looked like. He was constantly encouraging. He gave me my first sense of being an athlete. He even showed me what it was like to be a father and maintain a family. He would often have barbeque parties at his home and invite some of his players. Ironically, this was at the same time that my family barbeques were coming to an end because of my father's addiction. While I was seeing at home how things can fall apart, Coach Gunder was teaching me what it took to hold them together.

I've been sharing about football coaches to this point, and while most people know me because I played professional football, I was also a basketball player in my youth. Honestly, while I moved up and down over time in terms of skill levels in both sports, I was probably a better basketball player than football player. When I reached middle school, I found myself being coached by a two-man team who coached both sports. Coach Jackson and Coach Joyner came into my life at the same time and I'm so fortunate they did. It would take the two of them as men to fill the void being left by my father.

Early on, there was a moment that would become so important for everything else that would happen in my life, I wish I could have fully appreciated its importance at the time. The good news is that it so immediately started to change my life in a positive way that by the time it sunk in mentally it had already been at work practically.

Even though I was young, Coach Gunder had given me a bit of swagger. While playing football for him I had been both a quarterback and a running back, two high-profile positions, at least one of whom touched the ball on almost every play. Those who know football know that there is only one person who touches the ball on every play and that person plays the least glamorous position on the team. That position is center and that is precisely the position the coaches wanted me to play.

I wanted none of it. If playing football for these guys meant taking a step backward in terms of prestige and image, I would find some other way to occupy my time. Maybe I was thinking I could hang out on the streets with my dad after school or maybe I wasn't thinking anything at all. Perhaps it was as simple as telling myself, "If it's not going to be your way, then it's not going to be." Whatever the case, after learning that my position was set to be center, the next day I decided to skip practice. I was walking home along what was certain to be my life road to nowhere when Coach Joyner pulled up alongside me in his old station wagon.

The coach jumped out of his car and confronted me on the sidewalk. After he asked me in some form just what the hell I thought I was doing, and after I tried to explain myself, he said to me, in a voice that provided no room for discussion or dispute, "Get in the car. I'm not going to let you be a quitter." You can guess the rest. I got in the car and I played center that year. I played that damn inglorious position so well that I was named outstanding lineman at the end of the season. Without Coach Joyner chasing after me, the only award I would have won that season was for outstanding vagrant or scofflaw. Every single thing that has happened in my life since turned on that moment.

That moment was an unwitting first step to me learning to be a champion. The coach would not let me make being a part of a team be just about me. I reluctantly accepted my role. I performed in that role at my highest possible level. I wasn't self-sacrificing, I was self-improving and as I did, I lifted everyone around me. I became better, they became better, and we became better. Nobody becomes a champion on their own, but it's only through their own choice that they can make the decision to act and to become a champion.

Another side note, for those who work with young people. There are occasions where we can see a young person making a poor choice and be tempted to say to ourselves, "Well, they will either figure it out or they won't. It's their problem." While that is true on its face, we can find ourselves using it as an excuse to not intervene, to not go that extra mile to help that young soul. I'm not suggesting you can fix every kid in every circumstance. I do, however, want you to keep the story I just shared in mind and use it to help you decide when you should maybe jump into your station wagon and chase down that kid who might be about to throw their life away.

Coach Joyner and Coach Jackson also coached the Lakeland High School baseball team. They would take me with them to practice and they would pay me to shag balls that went out on the street. They made me think that they were giving me an opportunity to earn money. They tricked me—what they were really doing was keeping an eye on me, knowing that in my circumstance any sort of idle time was truly the devil's plaything. They were going to fill my life with sports so I couldn't fill it with anything else. Coach Jackson, who drove the polar opposite of a station wagon in his orange VW Beetle, used to come to my house and pick me up for various activities just to make sure I didn't get distracted along the way. That was both specific to the place I was heading at the time and a metaphor for not letting my life get off track.

I mentioned that basketball was my other sport. But whether or not I could have continued on past high school as a dual athlete, like the Florida State phenom a few years my senior, Charlie Ward, a Heisman Trophy winner who went on to play in the NBA and was drafted by the Milwaukee Brewers in baseball, I'll never know. I eventually made the choice to focus on football. Before the choice, however, I was a serious dual athlete and very serious about basketball.

My eighth-grade year was the nadir of my basketball life. I didn't just ride the bench, I wore a seat mark into the end of it. I thought I was better than what my playing time reflected and I was vocal about it. My teammates laughed at me and the star of the team irked me. While I thought I was better than was recognized by others, I decided that my only solution was to become so much better that nobody could ignore it. I resolved to prove that I was not only better than they thought I was, but also better than the star player on the team.

One of my maxims has become "polished practice leads to perfect performance." The rule I live by was born out of my frustration in eighth-grade basketball. I started practicing. Really practicing! I would be out in the street in front of our residence dribbling the basketball so late into the evening that my mom and brothers couldn't stand the sound of the ball on the pavement a moment longer. While I may have been committing the round ball version of waterboarding to my family and neighbors, I was more concerned with what I was doing. I was determined to be better and I was determined to prove wrong everyone who thought that seat at the end of the bench had my name permanently engraved on it.

What I was teaching myself, outside on the street in the late evening hours, was the importance of proving something to yourself and to others. Attending to the latter is being willing to force others to take notice. You can't prove something to someone else if they can't see it, and you can't just hope that they'll see it by stumbling upon it. You have to be willing to put yourself in front of them and show them. There's a time and a place to scream at the top of your lungs, "Hey! Look at me!" I knew this was going to be one of those times as I sharpened those basketball skills.

Most people have an image of who they are and who they aren't. The people around them also have an image or perception of them. Often, people let themselves get passed over in life simply because they're willing to accept that spot. I once asked a coach I knew and respected if he thought he would coach in the NFL. My experience with him certainly indicated he was qualified. His response to me was, "If it happens, it happens." While there isn't anything morally wrong with that mindset, it's not the kind of mindset that will help you win.

Sitting at the end of that bench, I could have accepted my role. It would have been easier for me than for most because I also had football. Who needs to be a standout at everything? I was learning that I just wasn't wired that way. I was developing an inner need not just to work hard, but to make sure that other people would notice the results of my hard work. I wanted my coach and my teammates to perceive me as a superior basketball player. I knew it wasn't enough to practice and become one. I had to make sure I did everything I could to make certain they took notice.

That particular lesson is one that every person can benefit from learning. I bet you know someone, even someone you see in the mirror, who likes to say, "I'm better than the other folks in my department. Why can't anybody see that?" The question that they, or you, should be asking is, "What am I doing to make people notice me?" Hard work isn't always enough. Don't ever leave the discovery of your own greatness by others subject to chance. Make them take notice!

There's a sort of catch to this: wanting to get ahead and be recognized has to come from a position of being ready to contribute and not just a feeling that you should be given the opportunity. You always need to ask yourself: do I want this promotion to bring value to the team, or to my ego? If the answer is the team, you're ready. If the answer is your ego, check your premise.

I did just that. I knew I was ready to bring value to the team and I was determined to make everyone take notice. I got better and I got in the face of my coach and my teammates and in so many words said "watch this."

I became a starter the following season and never looked back.

When I reached the JV level in basketball, life presented me with another occasion to make a choice and learn a lesson, a couple of lessons, actually. A situation arose that forced me to deal with a conflict that often comes up in life when you're faced with having to make a choice, where no matter what you decide, you're going to experience loss. *Star Trek* fans might know this as the Kobayashi Maru. The rest of us simply refer to it as a no-win scenario.

That season, our JV team was particularly talented and our varsity team was, well, not quite so talented. It's common in high school sports, either with an especially talented player or when the varsity team is struggling, to bring someone up early to the varsity level. We had both scenarios at work that year. To compound the matter, there were several of us on the JV team good enough to be called up. Not wanting to break up our core group, we took a pledge that none of us would accept an invitation to move up to varsity. We were committed to stick together.

As we expected, the invitations came. When they did come from Coach Alvin Jones, the other guys said no and honored our pact. I said yes and moved up. That's right. The guy who is writing a book about winning, and who has as one of his principles to protect your name and your word, very self-servingly broke his word to his teammates and did what was in his personal interest. Sound bad? Do I seem like a hypocrite? Stay with me while I explain without rationalizing.

When I was sixteen, I didn't have a system. I was a kid who was in the process of unwittingly building a system. The knot I felt in my stomach when I betrayed my word to my teammates was part of the trial-and-error process of life. The move up to varsity worked out very well for me, in terms of my athletic progress, but it never felt right. I don't view the move as having been a mistake. I did make a mistake, however. The mistake was making the pledge in the first place.

Today, as an adult with the benefit of that experience behind me, I live by a set of principles. One of those is simply to not make commitments you can't, or even might not, honor. When you're young, it's easy to fall into the trap of going along to get along. It's very difficult for a young person experiencing peer pressure to say, "You all do what you want. I'm not going along." This is true about avoiding drug use, going on a wilding spree, or even promising not to move up to varsity. A young person makes a promise they may not be able to keep, or even have no intention of keeping, because it's comfortable and expedient in the moment.

Of course, it isn't just young people who do it. We all know adults who are guilty of the same behavior. The difference is that the young person has a bit of an excuse. They're still developing as people. An adult has less to hide behind when they break their word.

Today, I have the confidence and clarity to not make promises I know in advance that I won't keep if the situation changes. I deal with things up front. In accepting the offer to move up to varsity, I benefited from making a bad choice I would never have had to make today. In my world today, I would have looked at my teammates when the pledge was being discussed and said, "I love you all like brothers, but I can't tell you that I'm willing to turn down an opportunity to advance my career. You're going to get 100 percent of me as a teammate, but if I get a chance to go, I'm going to take it."

The moral compass I have as a man today was not yet with me as a boy. It was under construction. I didn't make a mistake back then; I just made the right decision in the wrong way. Protecting my name and my word have become foundational for me and those principles serve as the friction between winning and winning at all costs. Today I sometimes have to make decisions and walk away from opportunities that would be winners for me. They would also require me to break my word. The difference between me then and me now is that today I'm very careful about giving my word to someone. I do it with greater caution and deeper thought. Once it's given, there are no take backs.

The move up to varsity came at a personal price and taught me a lesson. It also helped me learn the value of taking a risk. Recently, I was at a basketball game with my daughter and a very good freshman came on the floor for the varsity team. When my daughter asked me about how that works, I explained that sometimes talent allows a younger player that opportunity and if they take it, they usually get to become a starter the rest of the way through school because they become a known commodity to the coach. I spoke from experience. This was what happened to me.

Learning the value of risk taking helped encourage me to do more of that in life. Conversely, learning about the collateral damage that can come from your personal decisions has caused me to try to minimize, or completely avoid, those in my life. Trial and error. Winning through losing.

You know me as a football player, so let's go back to football. When I was heading into my junior year, the success I was having in basketball translated into confidence on the football field and everywhere else. I was learning that success and winning were invasive and contagious. Win here, win there, and win everywhere. Nothing seemed impossible to me anymore. I did seem to have more confidence in me than others did, as evidenced by the fact that when the starting quarterback on our team was injured at the start of the season, Coach Ernest Joe was heard saying, "If I have to start Desmond, I'll get fired."

Well, he did have to start me and he didn't get fired. I knew that I had something to prove, but I also knew it was mostly just to myself. I became the only person against whom I was competing. Tuesday's me was only competing against Monday's me. For the first time in my life, I felt like people were looking to me for leadership and guidance and I fully embraced that role. By the end of the season, the coach who thought I was going to cost him his job presented me with the coach's award. There is no better way to demonstrate accomplishment than there is by turning a skeptic into a believer.

The winning attitude I was developing would show itself in different ways. One of the things I noticed was that I wanted to be "the man." I wanted the ball in my hand at the end of the close game. In the past, I had always been willing to be the person who took the proverbial last shot. Now I *wanted* to be that person. If I had always been willing to, what exactly was this difference I was experiencing now in wanting to? It took me a little more life to figure it out, but I ultimately came to understand it.

Almost everybody is willing to take a chance at being the last-second hero. If the coach, or your boss, turns to you and says, "You're up," then the tendency is to indicate you're willing and to give it a try. It's an assignment. You're part of a team. You'll take it and do the best you can.

The person who *wants* that last shot, or that tough assignment, is the person who's willing to fail. That's the person who steps up and says, "Pick me." They're not saying it because they're convinced that they'll succeed; they're saying it because they know they can handle it if they fail. True confidence comes from knowing that you can fully handle failure. In my later years of high school, I was attaining that level of confidence. I wanted to be "the man" in every instance because I knew I could handle whatever came. I didn't know if my teammates could, but I knew I could. Leadership became my role. It became my obligation.

That kind of last-shot leadership, like winning, is not a talent. It's a skill. Anyone can be taught and, in fact, I believe a person *has* to be taught. If I hadn't been given those early lessons by Coach Jones, Coach Joyner, Coach Joe and Coach Jackson, then I likely never would have become that go-to guy. If I hadn't had them, then it would have taken some other person, or people, to step into the role they played. It would have been hard to count on and I'm so grateful all of them were there to help shape me and teach me how to be a leader, through watching them be leaders.

There are two moments from my senior year of high school that will stay with me for as long as I live. The first is "senior night" during the high school football season. The second is "senior night" during the basketball season. Interestingly enough, senior nights are usually bigger deals for parents than they are for athletes, who can be kind of embarrassed to have to hold mom and dad's arm and walk out in front of their friends. Plus, they just want to play the game they're there to play. In my case, however, whatever the senior night experience was for my parents, it was much greater for me.

Football first. Until senior night, my dad had never come to one of my games. On that night, absent in his addiction and absent in his vision lost to a shotgun blast, my father showed up, alongside my mother. It was the first time the two had been present together at one of my games. Most importantly, the man who had been the least present in my life, and who was needed the most, had finally arrived.

Having my father finally present made me feel complete. I needed my dad to be part of my life. There are a couple of different schools of thought as to what a person needs to make it in this world. One is the characterization of the self-made man. This is the person who doesn't need anyone but themselves, is completely self-reliant, and looks inward only for the necessary motivation. They become, in effect, a one-person team. I understand and respect that position and I know many great people who swear by it.

For me, I believe that people need a team. People need help. That team can have a hundred members or just a few, but it needs to be a team. I had to have my father on my team in order to fill out the roster and to have the position strength I would need in order to win. This senior night football game was the moment when I re-signed him to a long-term contract.

Moving the calendar forward a few months, it was time for senior night at the basketball arena. This time only my mom was in attendance and the ceremony, which included announcements and pictures, was to be before the start of the game. When it was time, my mom was nowhere to be found. I knew how hard she worked and how dedicated she was to all of us kids so I was less upset than I was concerned that something may have happened to her. When the ceremony was over and the introductions were complete, the game was set to tip off. Just at that last second, my mom came into the gym. We paused the start of the game and I got to have my picture taken with her. To this day, it's the only photo I have on my desk.

The significance of that moment was that it represented the sum total of all the thousands of moments that had come before with regard to my mom and her commitment to us. I have no way of knowing what she had to do to get to that arena that night. Her life wasn't easy and I'm certain that night wasn't easy, but with that being said, she made it. She didn't look at her watch and say, "Well, I tried." She got there. She always got there. Her word, her commitment, her motivation, her passion, and her relationships with her children, all of it, was on display. Is it a coincidence that my principles for winning mirrored in her life and that night? I think not. She isn't part of me. She's all of me.

I had navigated my way through high school. I left it with mom still at my side, dad back at my side, and a solid cast of family, friends, and coaches with me, as well. I had my team. It was time to see if I could take winning to the next level. It was time to go to college.

If I didn't already have some swagger heading into the college recruiting process, I certainly got it during the process. Lots of schools wanted me (with the notable exceptions of Florida State and Miami, or as they like to refer to themselves in a haughty manner, "The U"). Those snubs aside, I had lots of offers and I ultimately narrowed the choice to two schools, Virginia Tech and Wake Forest, both of which I "kind of," well, maybe just a little, told the coach that I wanted to go. I had stopped short of giving my word, but I certainly implied my word.

Not a problem. Mom would make the decision for me and then I could simply tell one of the two coaches it was what my mom and family wanted. I'd have an escape hatch and could save face. Unfortunately, what my mom was about to teach me was what my father had already learned in recovery: it's hard to save your face and your ass at the same time. Mom wouldn't make the decision for me. She basically said that it was my future and my choice. Whatever I decided, I was only going to have myself to blame when informing the non-selected coach.

In leaving me on my own, mom did me a favor even though she didn't realize it at the time. Everyone knows I chose Wake Forest. This meant I had to call the coach of Virginia Tech, a coach I had already told in so many words I was going to pick his program, and tell him I had a change of heart. It was a tough call, but I made it. I think I was fine on the phone, but the coach's reaction was a different story.

"I thought you told me you wanted to be a winner, son? You're never going to be a winner at Wake Forest. Doesn't that matter to you?" That was the coach's reaction to the news. He demeaned me and my choice and tried to make me feel like I was somehow betraying myself, and him, by not deciding to be a Hokie. I immediately realized that he was angry at me for not making the best decision for him. Wake Forest's coach, Jim Caldwell, by contrast, while happy with my choice, wanted to make sure I was certain that choosing his school was what was best for me. It was a tale of two leadership styles portrayed in two simple phone calls.

Years later, I learned that my influential basketball coach and role model, Coach Jones, had an especially gifted athlete, whose name you might recognize, who wanted to play basketball for him instead of wrestle, a sport in which he had a chance to be tops in the state in his weight class. When young Ray Lewis told Coach Jones that he didn't need to wrestle because he was already playing football, Coach Jones convinced him he was making a mistake. Wrestling would provide Ray with a chance for great achievement and advance his career. Lewis went on to wrestle instead of playing basketball and he won the state title. He's also had a few other achievements across the years.

Coach Jones did a similar thing by encouraging me to pursue football at the college level, despite his love for basketball and his assessment of my talent. Like Coach Caldwell at Wake Forest, these men were true leaders. They recognized that being a leader meant getting the people who looked up to you to understand their own strengths and then helping to give them the courage to pursue their own dreams. Leadership isn't about you. It's about those you lead.

Early on at Wake Forest, I got a big wakeup call. After being the BMOC (the old-timer acronym for big man on campus) in high school, I was suddenly surrounded by people who were just as good as and a lot better than me. I was coming in planning to be a receiver, which was a position I had never played but one at which I was committed to succeed. I had put on thirty pounds of mostly muscle since my senior year and was ready to go when summer camp started. At least I thought I was ready to go.

The first two weeks were brutal. Some guys didn't make it. It was kind of like Officer Candidate School in the military, where some recruits submit their drop on request

(DOR) in the first few weeks because they decide it's just too tough. I would listen to young men, my peers, on the phone home and literally crying to their parents. Because of that, I refused to call home during those first couple of weeks. I was afraid that if I did, I might end up submitting my DOR. I wasn't going to voluntarily put myself in a position that would increase the likelihood of me losing.

That period was a real learning experience in terms of self-awareness. People, especially men and ultra-especially alpha men, try to block out their emotions. They think it's a sign of weakness to let them surface. Blocking your emotions, however, isn't the answer. Just like a steaming pot with the lid held on too tightly, they will surface and explode if you suppress them. The key is to identify and recognize them and then be able to manage them through awareness. My not calling home wasn't suppressing my emotions; it was acknowledging their presence and not letting myself succumb to them.

Not calling home for a couple of weeks allowed me to experience four years of incredible success. One sign of success—though not necessarily the best one—is when somebody takes the time to make you a Wikipedia page. I have one, and the section pertaining to my collegiate career reads as follows:

> [Desmond Clark] was a wide receiver and caught at least one pass against every ACC opponent he faced. He was a two-time second team All-ACC selection, a two-time team MVP, and finished his career as the ACC all-time leading receiver with 216 receptions for 2,834 yards (13.12 yards per rec. avg.) and twenty touchdowns.

How would that entry read if I had allowed my emotions to overcome me and called home? Would there even be a Wikipedia page about me? The lesson I learned, which translates into so many difficult situations we face, is this: why call home if you already know you're homesick?

As my collegiate career progressed, I continued setting goals for myself. Being in the NFL was not one of those goals. It was a dream, but not a goal. There's a difference. Dreams are aspirational and something you almost literally just imagine as a possible outcome. Goals are specific, measurable, and attainable. At the outset, my first goal was simply not to fail. I wasn't going to have to go back. I wouldn't let my mother down and I wouldn't become my father. I wasn't going to end up working at the car wash where all it ever does is rain. By the end of camp my freshman year, I knew I could check that one off the list.

Moving forward, my goals were specific and sequential. I wanted to become better than the person in front of me on the depth chart. Check. I wanted to be the best receiver on the team. Check. I wanted to be the best offensive player in the ACC. Check. I wanted to be among the very best overall players in the ACC. Check.

In setting goals, I visualize the steep side of a mountain with a series of terraces. I look up, see that next ledge, climb and pull myself up, catch my breath, and climb to the next one. That's what I did at Wake Forest. Each "made it" that came out of my mouth was followed by the word "next."

When does a dream turn into a goal? When it no longer seems aspirational but instead becomes attainable. Between my junior and senior years, I did some inquiring. I learned that if I left college right then, I had a chance to be either a fifth-round pick or so in the NFL draft or at least to be invited as a walk-on free agent to a number of teams. I could play in the NFL. I did just enough checking to make sure that the dream could, in fact, become a goal. I returned for my senior year at Wake with a brand new goal in mind. While I might have been a hardworking and driven young man, I wasn't delusional. I knew the difference between fantasy and reality. The NFL was now a real opportunity for me. All I had to do was set a goal and achieve it. And I had learned plenty about that already in life.

My senior year wasn't just a smooth ride toward draft day. For the first time in my career, I got injured. I had missed two games with a knee injury, one of which was our big game with Florida State, which was supposed to provide me with a highly visible stage on which I could show my skills to NFL scouts. I was frustrated but not discouraged. I worked hard to come back and I kept my goal in mind. Nothing about missing two games could change the reality I had learned existed when I had made those inquiries the previous summer. I was going to get to the NFL.

The 1999 draft was not going to be great for tight ends. There were two ranked ahead of me by talent experts. My agent told me that if things went well, I could be drafted somewhere in the fourth round. If I wasn't drafted by then, all bets were off. Well the fourth round came and went. Not only was I not drafted, neither were the other two tight ends ranked ahead of me! Finally, in the sixth round the call came from Coach Mike Shanahan and the Denver Broncos. I was going to get picked. The other two tight ends had not been picked yet, and they ended up not being picked at all. I was grateful and humbled but I wasn't lucky. Too much hard work had been put in leading up to this moment for it just to be luck.

When the note came on the screen saying that the Denver Broncos use their sixth-round pick to select me from Wake Forest, my family room did not erupt in some deafening celebration. I looked immediately at my mom and saw this sort of simple smile spread slowly across her face, almost the way you can see water gradually soaking through a paper towel laid over top of it. It was twenty-two years of her commitment to excellence just slowly seeping through from her inner soul to her exterior. I felt it. I felt her. In many ways, this was her moment to savor, not mine.

Me? I sat and let the tape play in mind from the past twenty-two years. In that moment, I knew that nothing was over and everything in my life was just beginning. I couldn't help but think of what I had accomplished and what I had overcome. I felt proud. I earned that and owed it to myself. I took it in for more than just a few moments.

Then those moments passed. I had work to do. It was on to the NFL and a whole new level of challenge I couldn't even imagine. I was up for it. I was ready to continue winning. I had a lot more lessons to learn, but the ones I was bringing with me were going to get me off to a great start. The rest of this book will show you how I took what I had learned growing up in Lakeland and combined it with my NFL experience to come up with a winning formula for life that I believe is suitable to anyone.

CHAPTER 4

PROTECTING YOUR NAME AND YOUR WORD

> A good name is more desirable than great riches; to be esteemed is better than silver or gold. Rich and poor have this in common: The Lord is the Maker of them all. A prudent man sees danger and takes refuge, but the simple keep going and suffer for it.
>
> —Proverbs 22:1

Integrity. Reputation. Image. Character. Perception. Identity. Brand awareness. Each of these terms describes how you are represented in the minds of others. It's the way that people think about you. It's entirely about what they have come to conclude about you through interaction and observation. While you might have ideas about who and what you are, it's the thoughts others have about you that have much to do with your ability to win in life.

The bad news is that you can't get into someone else's head. If you tried, you'd be out of your own mind! You can't control someone's perception of you. The good news is that it's almost entirely within your power to shape and influence their thoughts. The most powerful tool available to you, in helping to imprint a positive image about you in the minds of others, is protecting your name and your word.

I've already shared the story of my father's drug addiction. Because of how young I was, I can only imagine just what that was doing to my family's name behind the scenes. How were my mother's friends and coworkers talking about us? How about the teachers and administrators in our school? What about the corner grocer or the neighborhood pharmacist? My brothers and I were oblivious to it at the time but it must have had a negative impact.

I also shared the story about how when I was in high school, I broke my word to my teammates and accepted an invitation to move up to the varsity level after pledging to them I wouldn't. This certainly isn't the kind of behavior I'm going to write about in this chapter as a model for keeping your word.

I'm mentioning these two examples again in order to let you know that the road for me with regard to protecting my name and my word hasn't been an easy one. Like everyone else, I've experienced adversity and learned through some personal trial and error. The word *learned* is the key. The purpose of this chapter is to share what I've learned, not what I've always known.

Create Your Own Essence

One word I didn't use at the opening of this chapter was *essence.* I didn't use it because it's the special one I like to use to emphasize the overall importance of your name and your word. Those two elements create the essence of who and what you are in the minds of others. The word essence has a meaning but it also has a feeling. There's a kind of aura to it that transcends some list of "words that would describe Desmond." It's tangible and intangible. We all have experience in asking someone why they do or don't like someone and they answer, "I can't quite put my finger on it." That's essence! While they might not be able to put their finger on it, you can. It's largely because you either have, or haven't, protected your name and your word.

Your essence is the sum total of everything about you. It's the combination of how you treat people when you're engaged with them and what they observe about you as they watch you operate. This idea of personal essence is no different than the brand you try to build as a business. Sure, you can try to define it, declare it, and shout it from a rooftop or a Super Bowl ad, but in the end, people will draw their own conclusions about you based on how you or your business engage with them directly and how they see you operate when you might not know they're looking.

The essence of you or your brand needs to be one that creates a positive emotional reaction in people. That doesn't happen on its own and it doesn't happen without follow-through, consistency, and effort. Nike can say "Just Do It" all they want. If they don't follow through with backing up their name and the word they give to the public regarding their products' performance, then their slogan would quickly change to "Nike Didn't Do It" in the minds of customers.

Acting with Intentionality Will Keep You Focused

One of the keys to protecting your name and your word is acting with intentionality in everything you do and in every personal or customer encounter you have. Whenever I go into a meeting, a social setting, or a one-on-one-engagement, I always keep in mind the question someone could ask right after I leave: "So, what do you think about Dez?"

My goal whenever I meet anyone, in any circumstance, is to give myself the power to be able to go back. Half of that process is acting in a way that others want you back, and the other half is acting in a way that doesn't make them want you to stay away. While those might sound like the same thing, they aren't. I had an experience in high school that illustrates the difference.

Heading into the district basketball tournament my sophomore year, Coach Jones stopped by the office to sign off on the team's official roster before it was sent to the tournament officials. All names for all players had to be on that roster or they would be ineligible to play. By his own recollection, Coach Jones didn't look at that roster as closely as he should have. My name wasn't on it and he missed the error. I couldn't play and the team lost the first game of the tourney.

Coach Jones felt awful. To this day he talks about how I could have reacted to the news but didn't. When he told me about his error he didn't know how I would react, he just knew it wouldn't be good. Instead I surprised him. All I said was, "It's OK, Coach. I know you didn't mean to do it." That reaction, or lack of reaction from me, made me stand out in Coach Jones's mind. I could have reacted in such a negative way that he wouldn't have wanted me around, even if it was because of his mistake. Instead, I took a positive step in protecting my name with Coach Jones, primarily because of what I *didn't* do.

Staying intentional about protecting your name and your word can help you stay focused not just in easy moments but especially in the tougher ones.

Choose Your Battles—Don't Let Them Choose You

Protecting your name and your word isn't always easy. In fact, it's often not easy at all. When someone behaves in a way that pushes you to your limits, it's natural to want to fight back. I say natural because it's truly part of our biological makeup. That visceral reaction we have is part of the well-known fight or flight response. By my nature, I'm inclined to fight more often than flee. I need to remind myself, however, that fighting comes with a price. It might just harm my name.

During my business career post-NFL I found myself in a dispute with someone for whom I had the greatest respect. We had made a business agreement that despite it being in writing, did not address the particular situation in which we found ourselves. During the dispute, both my name and my word were not only being challenged in our private exchanges, but also being brought into question with mutual friends and associates. Since I'm writing that your name and your word are key elements to winning, you might guess I wasn't pleased.

I was ready to fight. It took everything I had in me to resist the temptation to respond in the aggressive manner my emotions were directing me. I knew that if I dropped to that level, everything that was being wrongly said about my name would be seemingly confirmed to others through my actions. I resisted. By keeping my head, I was ultimately able to work through the dispute and restore the relationship with the person who had been such an influential figure for me, with my name remaining intact and no can't-take-back words. Today, when that person is asked, "So, what about Dez?" he answers in exactly the manner I'd hope for, with my name and word protected.

We all know the phrase "you made me mad." The truth is that nobody can "make" you anything. It's all about how you choose, or forget to choose, how to react. Each one of us needs to have our own standards. Most of us do. The problem is remembering those standards in a moment of confrontation or adversity. We have to keep reminding ourselves that we can spend a thousand days trying to protect our name and our word but we can lose all of those days with a single slip.

Corporations learn this lesson every day. Companies that have spent years trying to build their brand and create a specific corporate culture can find either one in jeopardy with a publicly revealed act that brings their word into question, which in turn leads to a doubting of their name or brand. This is when they learn that having an ample inventory on hand means more than just having lots of products on their shelves.

Constant vigilance in protecting your name and your word through committed and intentional action can help you to stockpile some good faith with the people in your lives or the customers in your checkout lines. This means that when you make mistakes or have that unfortunate incident that isn't even your fault, you might not lose the entire thousand days of good behavior. You may only lose eight hundred. You'll still have some rebuilding to do, but the work will be lessened. People and businesses who want to win and to remain in business need to constantly build inventory when it comes to their name and word.

When You Have to Fight, Control Your Punches

When I talk about the need to resist that fight or flight response, it doesn't mean you should never fight. Sometimes when the people you love and the principles you hold dear are under attack and threatened, you need to fight back. In fact, failing to fight back would likely damage your reputation. The key in fighting back is to do so while maintaining your rationality (at least a little bit more rationality than anger, which is hard sometimes). In 2015, I was put in a situation involving my stepson that forced me to fight back. I tried to do so by controlling my anger in the process. While I wasn't completely successful in that effort, there was enough at stake that I had to put my name on the line.

My stepson had been the victim of bullying and racial attacks at his high school which was located in the far-north Chicago suburbs. After various interactions with school officials, the situation ultimately led to a moment captured famously by TMZ, in which I launched into a profanity-laced speech in front of the cameras about what was happening in that school and to my stepson. It wasn't the way I planned it, and I'm neither proud nor ashamed of it. It happened the way it happened because a member of my family was under attack. I had to fight.

The reaction to my outburst was mixed. Some people applauded me, some condemned me, and some local officials tried to force me to leave the state! Conflicting views aside, I learned two things from the incident. The first was that making a strong stand against prevailing winds can sometimes make change. My stepson's circumstances improved. The other thing I learned was that I had invested enough time in building my name that for many who did view my actions negatively, I was able to quickly bounce back. I had inventory from which to draw. For those I lost forever, I feel that I lost them by protecting my name through standing up for my stepson. That's an acceptable loss.

Businesses need to keep in mind that sometimes they might need to step up and fight for something in the public square. We live in a time of greater social awareness in which companies are sometimes called upon to speak out and embrace causes that promote social justice and the general well-being. The effectiveness of any company trying to speak out on important issues will, in part, be determined by the reputation they bring into the fight. It will also be further determined by how they conduct themselves during the fight.

The question each individual and each business needs to ask before stepping in front of a TMZ camera is: *How much inventory do you have to spend and how are you going to spend it?* Another way to think of your inventory of goodwill is with the word *reputation.* Your reputation is directly related to the level of inventory you have or haven't built. We often hear the advice "you need to protect your reputation." This actually is backwards. A good reputation is nothing more than the balance of inventory you've built with others by honoring your name and your word. You don't protect your reputation in tough times; it protects you!

When you or someone you love is under attack, the first thing you need to do is to stop and force yourself to remember exactly who you are. In a moment of anger or frustration this can be difficult, but it's essential. When you fight back, you shouldn't be fighting with darkest part of yourself. You should be fighting back with all the light you carry and the values you hold. It's a lot like the Jedi knights who use The Force in *Star Wars*. Will you use your power to fight with good driving you or with evil? It's your choice. It's always your choice.

Your mom probably told you when you were in a conflict with kids at school, "Don't lower yourself to their level." Mine did. I tend to think about it in the more positive sense of "staying above the bar." You set a bar for yourself in terms of your conduct. In times of conflict, try to stay up above that, not even at, and certainly not below. Those viewing you will see and respect that. Your adversary might even take note.

The standards to which you hold yourself when in conflict, or even when you're not, should not be set in order to make people like you. There will always be people who don't like you, no matter what you do. The standards you set need to be set for yourself in order to make yourself a person worth liking. The same goes for creating the right kind of business climate. Make yourself the kind of company worth working for or buying from.

Not only do we have an obligation to ourselves to build our inventory and strengthen our reputation, we also have an obligation to others to make sure we don't lose track of what they have built, when they find themselves in conflict or other challenging circumstances. A friend of mine told me how a false story was deliberately spread about them by another person, as part of what turned out to be a fraudulent financial scheme. It cost them their position within a national organization and led to many people they thought they were close to turning their backs on them.

Eventually, when the scheme was exposed, the head of the organization sat down with my friend and apologized. In that apology he said, "I never should have believed it. I know you. I should have questioned what I was hearing."

To that, my friend replied, "Yes, you should have. After all the time we've spent together, you should have realized what you were hearing just wasn't right. It never should have made any sense to you."

That story had a good ending, but oftentimes people throw away relationships because they didn't bother to stop and think about the inventory someone else has built. They get caught up in the moment, or the drama, or the emotion surrounding an incident. We should never be too quick to toss away what we know about someone just because we've "heard" something. Your goal in protecting your name and your word and in building your reputation and inventory is to make it too heavy to toss!

Businesses and customers need to keep this in mind in this day and age because of social media information (good and bad), which is shared almost instantly and without much filter or fact-checking. We can hear something about a company, maybe your company, that may or may not be true, but regardless of its veracity, people only think about what they're hearing at that moment. We always want to have people consider a person or a company's entire body of work when evaluating who and what they are.

People and businesses need to remember that not everyone will take the time to do that. That means that, in times of adversity, we may need to remind friends and customers of who we are and always have been. We need to direct their attention to that pile of inventory we've built.

Don't Break Commitments and Don't Overcommit

One of my mentors in the world of business taught me that no matter how much you try to juggle in your life and no matter how much you might try to be different things to different people, in the end there's *only one name* on your tombstone. That means you need to be consistent in how you protect your name and your word so that one tombstone sends the one primary message you want it to send to everyone.

One of the keys to that is how you view commitment. While you can, and must, certainly make more than one commitment at a time, you can't allow yourself to make competing or conflicting commitments. You also can't let yourself, despite the temptation, replace one commitment that seems right at the time you make it with another commitment later on that might be more to your advantage.

This was the rule I broke in high school when I made a commitment to my teammates that I didn't hold to when opportunity presented itself. I learned a valuable lesson from that, which is to not be too quick to give your word and commitment to someone without first thinking it through. If you think you may break it, don't give it in the first place. You can't be a winner in life if you walk away from great opportunities. By the same token, the people around you can't be winners if you break your commitments to them. They might be relying on your commitment as a key to their own journey toward winning.

Being successful in playing team sports means lots of preparation and practice. We all know that the team has to be able to count on each and every member of the unit performing to the best of their ability. Anyone who joins a team is making a commitment to do what is necessary to help ensure the team's success. If they break that commitment, the entire team suffers.

Everyone knows that about sports, but what's the difference between sports and a business unit or your own personal circle of friends and family? There's no difference. Once you join, you commit. Once you commit, you have an obligation to honor that commitment. Honoring a commitment is a fundamental component to protecting your name and your word.

In the instant you make a personal or professional commitment, you start having a significant impact on others. They rely on your commitment when making their own commitments to people in their own affairs. If you break yours to them, then the dominoes are likely going to fall in their life. Certainly, your relationship is going to fall. This is why before giving your word to someone and before making a commitment, you have to try to look at the situation from their perspective and ask, "How will their life be impacted by the commitment I'm making to them?" Asking that question will help you avoid promising your teammates you'll stay on JV when you know you intend to move up to varsity.

Respect the time and the energy of others. It's simple. If you always keep that respect in mind you will make good commitments and you will honor them. Even something as small as being on time really matters. Time is the one thing that all of us are running out of together. Showing respect for people's time, by being there to start when you should be and ending when you say you will, is a gesture that people will notice and one that matters. Think about it in the opposite sense. How many people do you know who have a reputation for always being late? Now stop and think how you view that person with regard to their name and their word. They're likely not at the top of your list.

It can be easy to sometimes think that a commitment you make isn't a big deal. You may try to convince yourself that this particular one doesn't matter as much as some larger one would. When you do that, you're just trying to rationalize your way out of having to honor your commitment. Maybe you find it inconvenient, maybe another conflicting opportunity has presented itself (moving up to varsity), or maybe you just don't feel like it. I try to solve this problem for myself by saying there are no small commitments. There is no hierarchy. My word is my word. Period!

Recently I made an arrangement with my daughter that Wednesday and Sunday were going to be daddy-daughter time. No sooner had I made that commitment to her than I received an invitation to attend a pro sporting event as a guest of a potential client that I had been trying to meet with for months. I really had worked to get that meeting. Now, I had it! All I had to do was let my daughter know that we would do daddy-daughter night on Thursday that week.

But I had made that commitment to my daughter. I had no way of knowing just how much it would matter to her if I turned a Wednesday into a Thursday. Maybe she really was counting on that particular Wednesday night for a whole variety of reasons I couldn't even imagine. There was no way for me to get inside her head.

The good news is that I didn't need to get inside her head, because I was already clear within mine. I had made a commitment. There was no hierarchy. If I broke this, I was damaging her ability to rely on my word and I was setting a precedent that would make it easier for me to have an excuse for breaking my word in the future. After all, I did it once and nothing horrible happened. No matter how valuable that business opportunity was, the price I would pay for it would simply be too high. I told the client I'd love to go to the game, but I could only go if I could have *two tickets*.

Every business has standards for its operations and so do I. I'm always trying to achieve Six Sigma status in each area of my personal and professional life. That means I have to set clear standards and adhere to them under all circumstances, not just when it's convenient. In a later chapter, I'll talk about maintaining a commitment to excellence. Excellence is my standard in everything I do, including protecting my name and my word. I know if I start conveniently breaking my word, those exceptions will turn into my new standard.

I don't let myself off the hook for anything small when it comes to my name and my word—that's why I'm careful about giving them. I'd rather say *no* to someone today, than have to say *sorry* to them tomorrow.

Understand What It Means When People Count on You

When you're good about protecting your name and your word, good things happen. People want to be associated with you and want to do business with you. It's contagious.

In the world of business, even more so than in our personal lives, people need to know they can count on you. It's one thing when relationships are at stake, but people get to a whole new level of intense when profits enter the picture. A term with which more and more people have become familiar over the past decade is *supply chain.* This is the term used to describe everything that comes into a business in order for it to produce something that goes out.

Supply chain management has become a multimillion-dollar industry, filled with MBAs and algorithms.

In a nutshell, any company is only as strong as their ability to rely on their key suppliers permits them to be. When you're doing business with another company, you're part of their supply chain. If they can't rely on you, it costs them money. They might forgive you personally, but they'll remove you from their approved vendor list faster than you can delete a row in an Excel spreadsheet.

Conversely, when people can rely on you in business as part of their supply chain, they will want to recommend you to others and they'll do so enthusiastically. People like to get credit for doing something good. If you're the person who always does what you say you're going to do and you do it on time, then they know you're going to make them shine in the eyes of others if they introduce you. Protecting your name and your word isn't just the right thing to do—it's the profitable thing to do.

In your personal life, are you the kind of person who friends and family know they can count on to do what you say you'll do, when you say you'll do it? In your professional life, are you the supplier companies can count on to deliver on time and as agreed? If the answer to these questions is *yes,* then you're putting yourself in a position to win. If the answer is *no,* keep reading. Let's get you there.

The Best Damage Control Is Preventing the Damage

What causes us to lose inventory value when it comes to our name and our word? How does our reputation get damaged? We know that if we lie, cheat, and steal that nobody is going to trust us on a business or personal level.

I'm guessing that most of you reading this book don't think you do any of those things, and I'll go further to guess that you probably don't. That said, I bet everyone reading this book has had their name and their word lose inventory value at some point. Let's take a look at a few reasons that can happen that don't involve unethical behavior or nefarious intentions.

I've already mentioned that sometimes our commitments can become inconvenient to keep. That happens either because we're feeling lazy or because we're presented with some new opportunity that makes us want to break the first commitment. Both situations can be resolved by simply sticking to our word. Both of those situations can sometimes be avoided by learning how to say no.

Saying no is actually hard for most people to do. They don't like to say it because it makes them feel guilty, as if they're letting someone else down. It also can make you fear that someone won't like you because you said no. Finally, it can make you fear that you might not get something you want later on from someone because you said no to them today. Fear is a powerful thing.

What we don't stop to think about in the moment when we should really be saying no to a commitment, is what will happen if we say yes now, and break the commitment later? The typical person will get over the polite delivery of a *no* much better than they'll get over the reneging on a *yes.* Saying no to a commitment up front isn't impolite; it's courageous! It's having the honesty to say to someone, "I'd love to say yes, but if I do there's a really good chance that I'll let you down later. Your time and your commitments are way too important to me for me to risk letting that happen. Because I respect you, I have to say no." Being able to say no honestly and politely to someone, and letting them know you're saying it *because* you respect them, not because you don't, will help you protect your name and your word.

Another reason we lose respect for our name and our word is because we fail to respect ourselves and hold ourselves to a higher standard. If I see myself as dependable, reliable, and accountable, it won't be hard for me to make positive decisions. Conversely, it will be much harder for me to behave in a way that's contrary to those ideals.

Are you a person, or do you know someone who says, "I'm always running late. There's just nothing I can do about it." The person who says that, does that! This all begins with how you view yourself. If you accept that as your operating standard, it will become your operating standard. Other people will notice and it will become one of your tags.

I know a person who has a colleague who is so routinely late that the people in their office take bets on what time he'll actually arrive for a 9:00 a.m. meeting. They also sometimes lie about the start time of the meeting if they really want him to be there on time. This person's tag? "Always Late." When the people in the office chide him about it, his response is usually, "I know. I can't get anywhere on time. Things just have to start when they start." How do you think that impacts his name and his word with the group?

We can also damage our name and our word not just by what we say, or do, or think, but also by what we *don't* do, say, or think. This is where we get to misunderstandings caused by unclear communication on our part and inferences drawn by others.

I let people I deal with know that if I haven't clearly said something and they're not 100 percent certain, they need to ask me to clarify. I don't want people to assume I said something or think I implied a commitment. If I mean I'll meet with you on Saturday at 2:00 p.m., you won't have to guess; it will be crystal clear. So many times people accuse someone of breaking their word when they never gave their word in the first place. The other person just assumed that they gave it.

Consider this hypothetical situation that will probably sound familiar. You're wrapping up a call with a colleague you haven't seen in some time and you end by saying, "We should get together for lunch in a couple weeks." Your colleague replies, "That would be great. Let's do it." You hang up the phone and a month later when that person's name comes up in a meeting, you think to yourself: we were going to have lunch a couple of weeks ago but he never called. Guess I won't bother asking him again."

Sound familiar? I try my best to eliminate the kinds of inferences that can lead to my reputation being damaged by being clear and intentional in all my planning. When someone says to me, "Let's have lunch in a couple of weeks," I say one of two things. I either tell them that I just can't this month because of my schedule and they should reach out to me next month to see if it's possible, or I tell them to pull up Google Calendar and let's pick a date. My name and my word are too important to my winning to risk having them damaged because "let's do lunch" turned into "he blew off lunch."

If it's not on a calendar, it's not real. If it's not said and acknowledged, it's not real. Don't let yourself infer what others mean, and don't leave it to chance that others are making inferences about you. Most important, let people know that you're always going to be direct and clear with them about intentions and commitments. Give them permission to be the same way with you. Finally, make sure they know that if they are ever not clear, ask!

If you're person who doesn't lie, cheat, or steal as part of your daily regimen, and yet you find that people in your business or personal life sometimes share a perception of you that you don't think is right, then take a look at yourself in the context of the behaviors cited above. Do you say yes when you really should say no? Do you not hold yourself to a standard that forces you to hold to your commitments? Are you not specific enough with others in your communications about what you're going to do and when? These are easy ways to take steps to protect your name and your word in all of your dealings with others.

"It's Just Business" Doesn't Apply When It Comes to Your Name and Your Word

After reading these ideas, you might ask, "Desmond, this all sounds great. The problem is that in the workplace there are all kinds of people willing to do or say anything in order to get ahead. They don't care what they say, what they do, or who they step on. How am I supposed to embrace your ideas and win? Don't nice guys finish last?"

Just like the company you work for that has its own brand, you have one, too. Your business works at trying to tell the marketplace who they are. They attempt to reflect something similar internally with mission and vision statements. Once they are certain they have those properly defined, they create policies and procedures to try to get all employees to understand and embrace the desired company culture.

You need to treat yourself like your own brand and create your own personal culture. You need to do this with intention and purposefulness. If you don't, you're going to get branded anyway by others. Don't you want to define who and what you are? You can't surrender control of that to others.

Once you do that, you can position yourself as the constant against the shapeshifting of others. While coworkers might attempt to be "situational" in their standards and ethics, you will be the one that a supervisor or a peer can always "count on" to be the kind of person you have committed to being. You will have that standard of operations visible to everyone so they know exactly what to expect and when they can rely on you.

There are really two kinds of bosses. First there are the kind that see through the office politics and recognize the people who will do anything to get ahead of others; the win not just at all costs but win at any cost kind of employee. That is the kind of boss who will recognize your name and your word as being of great value and they will recognize and promote you for your attributes.

Then there is the boss who rewards the win at any cost people. They see the workplace as some kind of social Darwin experiment and they are just looking for survivors, no matter how they manage to survive. When that is the case, you have to ask yourself: What am I fighting for? Is this the kind of place I want to work? Is this the kind of boss I want to please? Fortunately, we live in a country where there are many opportunities to find the right kind of work environment with the right kind of supervisor who will appreciate an employee committed to protecting their name and their word. If those things matter to you, and if you're not in that kind of environment, pick a new environment. Ask yourself: Who am I trying to please? Others or myself?

I've stepped away from work situations in my life because I felt the atmosphere was toxic and what I would need to do to get ahead would force me to compromise on this first principle of winning. I'm not willing to do that. Some people might think that since I played professional football, anything after that is easy. It isn't. Starting out in the workplace I was just another worker trying to get ahead. Along the way I've had to make professional changes because of my principles. Notice I didn't say sacrifices. I would have made a sacrifice if I had not protected my name and my word in order to stay in a position.

Protecting your name and your word should not be thought of as a painful duty. Think of it as something that is virtuous and pleasant. Every day you complete where you can look in the mirror and honestly tell yourself that you held yourself to your own standard of operation today is a day that will end with you feeling good about yourself. Notice that when you look in that mirror, you don't see other people looking back at you. You see yourself. That is who you are.

Your challenge is to get the other people in your life to see what you see. It starts by protecting your name and your word.

Five Key Takeaways from This Chapter

- Define who you are (or others will) and live it.
- Your name and your word are your personal brand.
- Every interaction will influence how others see and value you.
- It's OK to say no, but if you say yes, keep your word.
- Your commitments have significant impact on others, so be reliable.

CHAPTER 5

THE POWER OF RELATIONSHIPS

> One who has unreliable friends soon comes to ruin, but there is a friend who sticks closer than a brother.
>
> —Proverbs 18:24

The seed for understanding the power of relationships was planted inside of me by my mother when I was just seven or eight years old. As I shared in an earlier chapter, when we were forced to move into the "black bottom" section of Lakeland because of my father's addiction, our life was anything but comfortable. We had no refrigerator and often no electricity. We really didn't have much of anything.

What did we have? Well, as my mother used to say, "As long as we have us, we have enough." To someone who has never actually had to live in abject poverty, that sort of statement might seem like a cliché. It can be hard to imagine that it's really true if you're reading this in front of a seventy-five-inch flat screen TV while sitting in a posh leather recliner. I can assure you, however, that one person's cliché is another person's only way to cling to hope.

That simple expression of my mother's was my way, and my siblings' way, of clinging to hope. Every day I knew that no matter how hard the struggle of life might seem, my relationships at home would get me through to the next day. If you can get to that next day, who knows what can happen.

The importance of all this didn't really fully strike me until I was in my twenties and I found myself in the Super Bowl as a member of the Chicago Bears. That team that year was special. We had a lot of talent, but we may not have been the most talented team in the NFL. What we did have were strong relationships as individual team members. That's what allowed us to perform at a level of excellence. We were winners.

I found myself thinking about how powerful those relationships were and I found myself remembering what my mother had said twenty years earlier. I decided that if I could find so much success, if I could be winning with just a handful of relationships, how much more successful could I be if I kept expanding the number of positive relationships in my life? In very simple mathematical terms, as an individual, I can only know so much. If I add twenty-five quality people to my world, I can know twenty-five times more. It was in that moment that I decided to make relationships a central part of my own personal approach to winning.

If we want to be winners in life, we need to be surrounded by others who can help us win. They can encourage us, teach us, provide us with resources, and help us in a whole variety of other ways. Sometimes they even do things for us that we could have done for ourselves, but because they stepped in to help we didn't have to do it alone. Relationships provide a sort of lever that lets us greatly increase our own natural strengths and abilities. There's only so much we can do on our own, but with the lever of relationships, we can move mountains.

My good friend and mentor Gary Rabine, who started paving driveways as a teenager and now owns a number of companies with a national footprint, likes to say that he would still just be a guy paving driveways if he hadn't figured out the power of, and need for, relationships. He knows the key role they've played in his entrepreneurial success. He also says that if you want to develop relationships, all you need to do is to remember to love people, to love your enemies, and the relationships will follow.

That might sound easy or impossible depending upon who you are. Either way, I want to spend some time focusing on how to build those key relationships in your life. After we do that, we'll look at how to maintain them, repair them, restore them, and even exit them. Only by coming at relationships from every angle can we develop a strategy for winning that maximizes their benefit.

Despite all of my incredible life experiences, and all the people I've had a chance to meet, everything I know about building relationships—the fundamental principles—came from my mother. Along the way I've had coaches say something better, or had a business colleague show me some more technical, procedural way to build relationships through networking, but nothing I've learned from America's best will ever replace the basic principles I learned from my mom. This section of the book is as much hers as it is mine. Here are my tips, compliments of the late and very great Rena Clark-Davis, on how to build positive relationships (I'm not going to help you build the kind that aren't positive):

Keep a positive energy. Nobody is drawn to a person who doesn't create a very positive aura around themselves. As I've written already, my mother's life had to be extraordinarily difficult. My siblings and I only saw the tip of it. We couldn't see what she was doing when we were at school and she was either at work or putting our home together. We couldn't see her at night when we were asleep and she was left all alone with her thoughts. What we do know is what we saw when we were in her presence. She was always the person with the smile and the kind words. She was the living definition of positive energy.

A friend of mine tells the story of getting to meet former New York City Mayor Rudy Giuliani in December 2001, right after 9/11. He asked the mayor how he managed to keep up the appearance of being positive through all the adversity. He said the mayor told him, "There are times I just want to put my head down and cry. But I know that everyone is looking to me for leadership. I can't let myself quit." That's the very essence of maintaining positive energy in difficult circumstances. Whether it's a mother in Black Bottom or a mayor of a city that's just been attacked, positive energy is contagious. It makes people want to have a relationship with you.

When Coach Ernest Joe took over as coach of the football team at my high school, the team had been 1-9 the year before. He told the team going in that he had a plan for success and that he was going to work with each player to make them believe in it. He focused on building positive relationships with every player and he turned that team and the entire program around. My relationship with him exists to this day and he is referred to in this book because of the positive energy he brought to his job. I never want to lose that relationship.

Add value for the other person. There's a sort of transactional nature to relationships wherein each person needs to feel that the other person adds some sort of value to their life by becoming a part of it. My mom was my mom so she was going to be in my life whether I liked it or not. Everybody understands how that part of the parent-child relationship works. The reason that my relationship with my mom was so strong, the reason I still wear pink every Tuesday to pay tribute to her valiant fight against breast cancer, is because of the value she brought to my life.

Her positive attitude every morning was what gave us the strength to go out the door and face the world. That is valuable. The fact that she worked so hard to make sure we had clothes and shoes that fit, that she exhausted herself in every way to give us what she could in terms of financial stability, that had value. The advice she would give us in difficult times to help us navigate the challenges of growing up certainly had value. The unconditional love she gave to all of us, well, that had the greatest value of all.

It's important to pause on that notion of love for a moment. As a Christian, the Bible plays a front and center role in my life. There is an expression that the Old Testament gave us God's law and the New Testament gave us God's love. I believe in that part about love and I also know that it might sometimes be the hardest part of the Bible to successfully incorporate into your own life. Some people are really hard to love! That said, if you can force your way to love others, if you can let them see that in you, in a world that is often harsh and cruel, that love will have great value and it will make them want to be in a relationship with you.

Be judgment free. My mom never tried to tell us who we were supposed to be. Each and every day she showed us by example who she was, but she let us be us. I know exactly what she was up to. She wasn't giving up on trying to shape us, she just knew that if she tried to force us to conform to what she wanted we would likely rebel the way most children naturally rebel. She wanted us to become our own person and she wanted any "conversion" we might make to becoming the kind of person she wanted us to be would be a voluntary conversion.

We live in a time when people can be very judgmental. There are so many divisions between people that for many just being able to have Thanksgiving dinner together is a struggle. Whenever you start from a position of thinking "since you aren't like me there must be something wrong with you," then you create a barrier to establishing a relationship. We can decide we don't want a relationship with someone before we even meet them simply because we've heard something about them that suggests they aren't exactly like us.

Social media has made this problem even worse for two reasons. First, we now have more people than ever before sharing publicly what they think about everything, even if they were frustrated or angry when they shared it, or if they didn't really stop to think it all the way through. Regardless, once it's out there, it's out there and we use it to make judgments about them without even talking to them. This makes it easy to judge them and discard them if they don't seem to agree with us or if we don't like what they said.

What is just as bad or worse is that employers can now use your social media content to judge you before they even interview you. This means that a very critical kind of relationship, one involving employment, might never have a chance to start because of the judgment someone might make from Facebook. It's hard to resist judging others when they're publicly sharing what they think and feel. It can seem like they want us to judge them.

If we want to have meaningful and positive relationships we have to resist the urge to judge others, especially in advance. If you're a Democrat and you get introduced to someone you know is a Republican, try to resist the urge to judge them. Instead, try asking them, "What do you believe in? Why do you believe it?" You might find some common ground. There may be lots of things on which you don't and never will agree, but that doesn't mean that having a relationship with that person would be of no value.

Encourage and challenge other people to be at their best. This should be the easiest thing of all to do. It means being a cheerleader without having to wear a uniform or risk climbing to the top of a human pyramid. It might be because it's so easy that we forget to do it. It might also be that because cheering for others isn't the same as cheering for yourself, that we sometimes let our egos get in the way.

My sophomore year of high school I was the starting quarterback junior varsity. We started the season without a win and then, to add injury to insult, I got my tooth knocked out and my jaw temporarily wired. I was out of action for the season. The very next game, with me there on the sidelines as cheerleader for my teammates, they actually won the game...without me! There was a great celebration but I wasn't a part of it.

On the ride home from the game I was silent and likely pouting a bit. My mother turned to me and asked, "Are you upset they won without you?" I don't remember exactly what I said, if anything, but I must have made it clear that I wasn't exactly "feeling the love," of the team's victory.

"These are your teammates. You should be happy they won without you," was my mom's reply to *my* uninspired reply. I've never forgotten that moment.

Coach Ernest Joe says that when he was coaching he was committed to following a kid in his program all the way through school. He would go to the student's house if he had to in order to give them the encouragement they needed to keep going and not quit. That kind of cheerleading made the students who played for him want not just to play then, but so many of us have stayed in touch with him over the years because we did not want to lose that relationship. Who wants to lose a cheerleader and someone who challenges you to be better?

Being that cheerleader is more than just telling someone that they can do it. It's getting them to believe that they can do it and helping to give them the strength to move forward. Everyone always wants to be giving people advice. The truth is, most people know what it is they should do or have to do, they just lack the willingness and courage to do it. Being that cheerleader, giving them encouragement and challenging them, gives them the power to act. It helps enable them to win. When you do that they will remember and they will want to have a relationship with you.

Be consistent and reliable. Remember the story I shared about my mom coming into the basketball game at the last minute of senior night? That is a great example of what I mean by being consistent and reliable. She never let us down. People are drawn to people they know they can rely upon. Conversely, people instinctively pull away from people that let them down. In your personal life, people that are not consistent and reliable cause you to feel hurt. In the world of business, people who are inconsistent and unreliable cost you money. Neither of those two things will build you relationships.

Consistent and reliable can sound like they are the same thing, but they really are quite different—complimentary but different. Consistent means that people know what they are going to get from you when you show up. Reliable means that they know you really are going to show up.

My mother showed her consistency in her approach to life even up to the moment of her death. She would say, during the course of her illness, “Don’t ask me if I’m all right. If I woke up this morning, you already know I’m all right.” Another line she used to use was, “I may have cancer, but cancer doesn’t have me.” My mother lived a life where she consistently expected nothing from anyone and never stopped a single moment to engage in her own private pity party. The Lord knows she had reason to be angry, bitter, and discouraged. She was never any of those things. Even in the months leading up to her death at a far too young age, she was consistent in her own take on life. No wonder so many people wanted a relationship with her.

Reliability is just as important as consistency. It doesn’t do anybody any good to know what to expect from you if they don’t know if they can expect it from you today. A friend shares that when his daughter was young they had the world’s greatest in-home babysitter to watch their child while they were at work. The quality of care she provided was very high with lots of love and nurturing. She was consistent in that regard.

So why did they fire her and sever their relationship with this super caregiver? Because every once in a while she just wouldn’t show up. Sometimes she would call at the last minute. Sometimes she wouldn’t call at all. Sometimes she wouldn’t even answer the phone. After giving her numerous opportunities because of her otherwise consistent performance, they fired her because she wasn't reliable. A relationship lost.

Be curious. You need to show people that you're interested in who they are and what they're doing. Another mentor of mine, a successful financial professional by the name of Manuel "Manny" Amezcua, likes to say that attention is the greatest currency in today's world. People have so many distracting and outside influences around them that it's easy to feel lost in the world. If you can truly pay attention to someone and let them know you're interested it will make them want to have a relationship with you.

Being genuinely curious about someone will allow you to focus on the question: *What do I have to offer to them that is of value*? If I don't let myself be truly curious, how can I discover what might be of value to someone else? I can't just decide what it is in advance based on what I know about myself. I have to learn it by coming to know them. Going all the way back to Dale Carnegie's lessons on "How to Win Friends and Influence People," we know how important it is to make other people feel you're listening and that you care. Being genuinely curious about someone gives them a chance to talk about themselves. Everybody likes to do that!

We think too often about being attractive to others. Showing interest and curiosity in other people will make you attractive. You will actively draw people to you. It's a key in creating relationships.

Be intentional. We live in a world today where there is so much connectivity (maybe too much based on some of the social media thoughts I shared), that not too many people think they need to have more "friends." Before you do the work you need to do to enter into a relationship, ask yourself: what have I seen in this person that makes me want to have a relationship with them?

There truly does need to be some sort of value proposition in a relationship and it needs to be felt by both parties. The value doesn't have to be the *same*, but both people have to perceive some sort of value and the value for both should somehow intersect.

As a former NFL player, I know there are people who want to have a relationship with me simply for that reason. For better or worse, part of our culture says that having a relationship with a former pro athlete is "cool." While that might be a great motivator for another person, for me that kind of relationship has little value. Our intentions would not be the same and would not likely be able to align. Being intentional in creating a relationship means not just understanding your own intentions, it means understanding the intentions of the other person, as well.

Maintaining Relationships

Relationships are not like collecting Hummel figurines or autographed NFL helmets. You can't just put them in a nice case and then have them on display to either look at by yourself, or to show off to others. Relationships require attention and maintenance in order to continue. I could use the metaphor of an automobile, but we want relationships to last longer than five years or fifty thousand miles.

How many times have you said in your life, "I wonder whatever happened to that person?" Usually we ask that question because we care about who that person is or was. We don't usually ask a question if we don't care about the answer. We live busy lives with lots of distractions, now more than ever. If we don't pay attention to our relationships, they can simply drift away. Said another way, from the recovery world of my father, we keep what we have only with vigilance.

What are the keys to relationship maintenance? I have a few and they're not complicated. That said, please don't be dismissive of their simplicity. If it were really easy to maintain relationships, we wouldn't be asking, "I wonder what ever happened to...." so often.

Set the terms. So many problems that lead to lost relationships could be stopped before they ever happen simply by setting the terms of the relationship up front and then resetting those terms as needed when things progress and change.

There are things I let people know right up front that are kind of "operational." I set my phone down at 9:00 p.m. I don't interfere with daddy-daughter time. I don't just hang out a lot. If I bring you to my home it's because I'm bringing you into a deeper circle of people. These are some almost mechanical elements of a relationship. They are boundaries, simple and basic boundaries. Letting people know these up front helps prevent misunderstandings from ever happening. Nobody calls me at 10:30 at night and wonders why I'm ignoring them. I'm not answering and they know it up front.

These kinds of terms are the easier ones to establish. The harder ones relate to letting people know what to expect from you in terms of emotional and time commitments. Generally speaking, people are not comfortable about setting limits with people because it makes them feel like they sound uncaring. Instead, they end up setting the limits anyway by just "not being available" and then they really come across as uncaring! One way or another, we end up setting limits. It's best to do it upfront.

This is one of the biggest mistakes employers make with their employees. Every employee has a job description, either formal or informal. The problem with job descriptions is that they tend to stop with just the mechanical requirements of the job. They don't make it clear what kind of boss you are and what the rules of engagement look like for someone working for you. Tell them what your boundaries are. Tell them what your weaknesses might be. Tell them what *not to* expect from you. While in this day and age we have to be careful about how we communicate with people in the workplace, it doesn't mean we shouldn't communicate. We just have to be a bit more thoughtful, careful, and precise than we used to be.

We also have to set the terms of the relationship as it progresses. People and circumstances change. Not only do we have to be aware of our own changes, but we have to be in a constant state of learning about the other person. We need to look for changes in their dreams, their families, their friendships and associations, and their values. Looking for these changes and discussing them with that person will help us to know if the rules of our relationship need to somehow change.

Be intentional. Another trick I've learned, this one from Manny, is to keep a list of relationships as a sort of "tickler file" for staying in touch. For those people who are not in my inner circle (family, close friends, immediate coworkers, and so on), I keep a "Top 50" list. Every Friday I look at the list and determine who I need to reach out to and how I'll reach out, whether it's by phone or email or another way. This way I don't lose track of people. I don't find myself asking whatever happened to so and so.

Now this list changes over time. There could be someone on that list with whom I'm negotiating some business arrangement. Perhaps after some effort, the arrangement fails to come together. In that case, it might not be necessary to maintain that relationship any longer. It may drop off the list, but always to be replaced by another person. The list stays at fifty.

While this system might not seem feasible for you, that's OK. The point isn't to have *my* system, it's to have *a* system. In order to be a winner, you can't let the maintenance of your relationships be a product of chance. Find a system that fits with your own personal habits, your technology, and the key elements of your life and work.

A special tip to business owners and managers. Be aware of office "cliques." These types of informal groups can undo relationships within your company very slowly and sinisterly. All the work you do to try to establish boundaries and set terms with your employees can be undone in the break room, at the water cooler, or at happy hour. Try to keep your door as open and inviting as possible. If your employees know they can come to you, it makes it at least a little less likely they'll go to someone else. As my mentor Gary Rabine says, "Saying you can't get close to your employees is a bunch of b@#%%##$s!"

Sometimes, no matter what we try to do to maintain a relationship they become strained. When that happens, just like that car metaphor I didn't want to use, they can find themselves in need of repair or restoration. Next I'll share thoughts on how to get a relationship back on track.

Repairing and Restoring Relationships

Recently I had a relationship that I mentioned in the previous chapter that was severely damaged. I already discussed how I did not want to lose my cool and damage my name in the process of addressing the problem. One of the key reasons I decided not to let that happen is because the relationship itself was worth saving! That's the very first question you have to ask when trying to repair or restore a relationship: Is the value here worth the work that will be required to fix the situation? If the answer is yes, here are some suggestions for what to do:

Determine if you both recognize the value. I already said you have to ask yourself if the relationship is worth saving. The person on the other side of that relationship and their answer to that question is just as important. How can you find out if the relationship is worth saving from their perspective? Try asking them! Never underestimate the power of a direct question. Sometimes, just asking someone if they think a relationship is worth saving can be enough to get the relationship back on track. When both parties acknowledge that *something* has to be done, the hardest part just *got* done. If you both feel that it's worth salvaging but more than just that acknowledgment is required, then get to work!

In business this can be very difficult. Business relationships almost invariably involve money and money complicates things. While the stakes are high, and while cool heads and rational action are most needed when money is involved, just money's mere presence can cause us to behave in the exact opposite manner. Make certain that the calculation of the value in the relationship not only includes the dollars that are on the table, make sure it also includes the ones you can't so easily see below the table in terms of time and energy costs to preserve the relationship.

Compromise. This has become a bit of a dirty word in today's world with people everywhere pointing to compromise as a synonym for weakness. When it comes to repairing relationships, compromise is an absolute necessity. You need to put yourself to the side and try to see and feel the situation from the other person's perspective.

Compromise does not mean surrender. It means that you're taking an honest look at the relationship and asking yourself, "Is this of so little value to me that I'm not willing to give up something of value to keep it?" Sometimes the answer to that question truly is yes. If it isn't yes, then get to work on finding that middle ground. To borrow yet another expression from my father's world of recovery, "sometimes you can only keep what you have by giving it away." When compromising, you may not have to give everything away, but something will have to go.

Finally, remember that if you're to the point where you're debating whether or not to compromise, it's likely that you've already decided it's worth compromising. You just have to work through your own stubbornness to finish the job.

Say you're sorry—and mean it. Nothing in the world can have more impact than a direct, clear, and heartfelt apology. We all recognize the fake kind, the kind where someone says, "I'm sorry if what I said offended you." Those kinds of apologies do more harm than no apology at all. Apologies need to be unequivocal. They also need to be specific.

A teacher I know told me that he tells kids there are two sets of two-word phrases that should never be used alone. Those two are "thank you," and "I'm sorry." Thank you for what? I'm sorry for what? Anytime you find yourself in need of repairing a relationship where you have not kept your side of the street clean then you need to tell the other person exactly what it is you're sorry for having said or done. Say the words! It only hurts during the moment you're saying them. It feels invigorating once they are out.

As an aside, regularly telling people exactly why you're thanking them might just be a good way to help maintain those relationships before they get in trouble.

People want you to acknowledge that you know what it was that hurt them. That's why apologies have to be specific. If you can't express it, then you don't really understand it. The other person knows that. Don't let yourself be afraid of being transparent and vulnerable. I'm a former professional football player. That is about as rugged a culture as you can find. It took some time, but I've learned to show my true self to others. If I can, you can.

You also have an obligation to take seriously the genuine apology of another. If you find yourself rejecting an apology, you need to question yourself. What is in you that is causing you to reject the extended olive branch from someone? Sometimes we reject an apology because deep down inside we might just be a coward. We might be afraid of giving someone another chance and then letting ourselves be disappointed all over again. Part of winning in life means having the possibility of losing. I'm willing to accept that risk. I'll accept a genuine apology.

Exiting Relationships

Sometimes a relationship needs to end. We don't live in a perfect world. Sometimes a relationship can't be saved, and sometimes it shouldn't be saved. When a relationship has to end:

Do it the right way. We don't ever want to burn bridges. It's only after we have just finished crossing one that we feel confident we will never have to go back. Things change. A time may come when we do have to go back. Besides, how you end a relationship impacts your name and your word. There is no reason to place anything at unnecessary risk. Leave the bridge intact, or at a minimum leave the pieces off to the side to be reassembled.

Remember that when you end a relationship you're impacting someone else's emotional state. You owe them the basic human decency of doing it right. This is something that is too often ignored in the world of business when terminating an employee. Someone who was your "star" a few years ago can suddenly be treated like a villain just because they didn't meet quota. You know what they say about karma? Remember that even when terminating an employee, take the writer Tom Wolfe's advice to heart: *Be what your grandmother taught you. Be a decent person.*

Don't just stop answering calls and don't stop returning emails. Oftentimes, the other person might not even realize anything was wrong. Man up (or woman up) and reach out to that person and let them know you're ending the relationship. Tell them why. Tell them that in order to stay on your own path to winning that you need to exit from this relationship. If you can be clear and honest with them, you will likely leave a door open to having that relationship restored someday. Maybe they can get back on your list of fifty!

Now that we have covered protecting your name and your word, and have shown the power of relationships, it's time to explore what it means to have a commitment to excellence. While that may seem a bit general to you, keep reading and let me show you what I mean by committing to excellence and how it will increase your opportunities for winning at life.

Five Key Takeaways from This Chapter

- As my brother Manny says, "Relationships are the most valuable currency."
- The quality of our lives is tied to the quality of people in our lives.
- To become valuable to other you have to add value to the relationship.
- Clearly communicate and agree upon expectations.
- Never burn relational bridges.

CHAPTER 6

MAINTAINING A COMMITMENT TO EXCELLENCE

> The will to win, the desire to succeed, the urge to reach your full potential—these are the keys that will unlock the door to personal excellence.
>
> —Confucius

Assuming you're reading this book in chapter sequence, you've just finished two chapters you probably thought were pretty challenging. I've shared the importance of protecting your name and your word, even in the most difficult of circumstances. Then I've tried to drive home the need to establish and preserve relationships and how it sometimes has to be done with people where it might be uncomfortable or even unpleasant.

It would be easy to look at a chapter on excellence and think: *This one will be easy. It's such an abstract word. This chapter is probably just filled with platitudes and lofty language.* Keep reading. Pursuing excellence is something that is easy to say, but not so easy to have the discipline for consistent follow-through. This chapter is designed to help convince you that a commitment to excellence matters, and to give you meaningful tips for successfully incorporating the principle into your daily life.

There is nothing inherently right about my choice of the word excellence. There are plenty of synonyms in *Roget's Thesaurus* and just like when I discussed protecting your "name," there are different words you could substitute. I use the word excellence because it came from one of my former NFL coaches, Mike Martz. Coach Martz came to Chicago and told us we were going to be excellent in every area. He used that word and reinforced that idea in every drill at every practice. The word, and the concept, stuck with me.

It's worth noting that under Coach Martz I didn't have my greatest success in the NFL. While I might have been pursuing excellence in my own personal space, the coach didn't see me as the best tight end and my playing time under him was limited. As frustrating as that was, and as much as I might have felt I deserved more playing time, I was able to separate my personal situation from what he was trying to accomplish for the team. That in and of itself was a powerful personal lesson for me to learn.

Coach Martz isn't the only NFL coach to try to create an atmosphere that pursues excellence. Most coaches do regardless of what label they choose. My friend and former NFL teammate, Byron Chamberlain was a Pro Bowl tight end who played on two Super Bowl winning teams while with the Denver Broncos. Those teams were John Elway's by way of public perception, but they were Coach Mike Shanahan's team behind the scenes. The teams were a reflection of Shanahan's version of "commitment to excellence."

Byron recalls Coach Shanahan addressing the rookie draft class by saying, "We're going to do things here one way, and one way only—first class! Everything will be first class." In Denver, Coach Shanahan would set standards, not only for performance levels, but for everything. There were standards for how the players would dress, how they would travel, even how they would eat! No aspect of team behavior was going to be less than first class in Coach Shanahan's mind.

Byron tells the story of the practice right before Denver won their first Super Bowl. In that practice, the offense did not have a single dropped pass. Not one! That is unheard of. Byron and his teammates knew then and there they were going to win the Super Bowl. Those "first class standards" of the coach had made the team excellent.

That word has come to sit on a slightly higher perch for me than do similar words that might be the result of a sustained high level of performance. For example, you can be successful without necessarily being excellent. Some people might want to argue about the distinction, but I ask you to not get lost in your own personal dictionary. Understand that when I use the word excellence I'm talking about the highest achievable level of performance. Use any word you might want, but don't lose that meaning. The best part of the word *excellent* is that anyone who hears it knows it's the highest possible standard.

Having a commitment to pursuing excellence and experiencing rewarding results from that effort is not related to class, or money, or anything that is necessarily visible to the outside world. Back when I was still playing football, I would look at my brother and his family. He had a job he loved, he was pursuing his passion of coaching, his family was healthy and happy; everything was excellent. I was making ten times the amount of money he was making but I was still trying to fully find myself in life. Nobody on the outside looking in would have guessed he was doing a better job of pursuing excellence than was his NFL brother.

At some point during my NFL career I stopped and looked back at how things in my life had gone differently depending upon whether I had, or had not, committed to pursuing excellence in the moment. I came to the quick conclusion that pursuing excellence was a key element to winning. Now I'll share what I've learned about how to pursue excellence and how you can incorporate those ideas into your own approach to winning.

Excellence: A Four Step Process

I learned after I left the NFL and started in the world of motivational public speaking that people like to have lists. Anytime you have the "Ten Rules for…," or the "Seven Habits of….," you're more likely to connect with people. They feel like they can find a way to remember what you're saying. In that spirit, allow me to share with you four steps for pursuing excellence that you can work into the overall five-step process for winning.

Step One: Dive into Self-Development

You have to be willing to invest the time into getting yourself ready to pursue excellence. Everything about mastering something in life involves an educational process. If someone wants to be a doctor, they study. If someone wants to be an auto mechanic, they study. If someone wants to be an NFL coach, they study. If you want to be excellent, you need to study, too.

Over time, I've become a believer in reading books just like this one. I'm always a bit surprised when I read something that sounds a lot like me, and I'm always spiritually and intellectually challenged when I read something I had not thought of before. While I was in the process of writing this book, I was busily reading others that are like it. No two are exactly the same because no two people have had the same set of life experiences that inspire them to share their strategy. What all books like this one share is the positive message and energy that they bring to the reader. They all help make you ready.

I encourage you to read and listen to messages that focus on helping you to become a better overall human being, not just a better performer in a single category or area. Some people try to commit to excellence in just a certain part of their life. They effectively compartmentalize their steps to winning. I think that only trying to pursue excellence, trying to win, in some areas but not others leaves you living a life that is incomplete. How can it ever be fulfilling to say, "I'm not pursuing excellence right now. I did that earlier today. I'm chasing mediocrity at the moment."

If you can focus on learning things that prepare you as a person, then you can more easily create a set of standards for pursuing excellence that are always with you and that you're always applying. I think that is a better approach than having to stop and remind yourself when you should or shouldn't pursue excellence.

Another key component of self-development is to find a mentor, or mentors, to help you with your progression—people to help you learn. A friend recently shared that he was in a meeting with a room filled with entrepreneurs who were all successful and who all took turns sharing their story of success. He said that the one common thread in the room was that every single one of them had at least one key mentor they had chosen, if not more than one. This isn't complicated. People who have already made it are able to share with you what they did to make it. You can "cheat" by learning from them directly what they may have learned on their own the hard way.

I've mentioned a couple of key mentors in my own post-NFL professional growth and development: financial wizard Manny Amezcua and entrepreneur extraordinaire Gary Rabine. Gary takes the notion of mentoring so seriously that he started an organization called True Mentors in the Greater Chicago area. True Mentors brings together young and aspiring entrepreneurs with seasoned and successful ones to give the upstarts the chance to learn and the ones who have made it a chance to give back. A common progression within the program is to have someone transition over time from mentee to mentor. The cycle of learning continues.

The key element to True Mentors success is the desire of the mentees in the program to continue their self-development. Never stop learning. Never stop making yourself ready.

Step Two: Set Your Goals and Standards

Pursuing excellence is a step that every person needs to take if they want to win in life, business, football, or anything else. What denotes excellence, however, is something that is different and unique to each person. You can't take my definitions and I can't take yours. Since you can't take anybody else's, that means you need to get to work, once you've had a little education, and set your own goals for excellence and set the standards for achieving those goals.

The first requirement in setting goals and standards is to create a vision of where it is you're going or who it is you want to be. You need to aspire to something. There's an old slogan that shows up on coffee mugs and office wall posters that reads, "Nothing happens, if not first a dream." As trite as that might seem, there is a lot of truth in it. The only thing that stops our movements from being completely random is intentionality. Why not move intentionally toward a vision we set for ourselves.

Once you establish that vision of what you want to be, it's time to move toward it to make it real. This is where it can get a little tricky and where you might encounter the chicken-and-egg problem. The good news with pursuing excellence in the quest to reach your goal is that unlike to logically unsolvable chicken-and-egg conundrum, the problem of moving forward can be solved.

What exactly is the dilemma? It's the need to determine what has to come first: action or belief. Some people will argue that if you don't actually believe in something, there's no way to get motivated and start. The very fact that you don't believe what you're aspiring to do is realistic or attainable will stop you dead in your tracks. That can be true, but only if you let it be true.

Let's use the example of someone with a weight loss issue. You may know this story firsthand, or at least secondhand. We are an overweight nation in a nation that is very weight conscious. That contradiction creates an awareness and attendant desire in a lot of people to lose pounds. They set a vision of themselves if not in a Speedo, then at least in a pair of yoga pants or a trim fit golf shirt.

Once they have that vision, they can set a goal of pounds to lose and they can create the standards they will apply to their weight loss process (diet, exercise regimen, etc.).

All set, right? Not necessarily. Some people stop before they start because they look at the vision they have for themselves, they see the weight loss goal number, and they just don't let themselves believe they can really make it. They quit before they start because they don't believe. That absence of belief leads to an inability to take action.

What if they were able to just take action? What if they had the ability to say to themselves, "I don't necessarily believe I can do this, but I'll start anyway." If they can just start to take action, and if they can create movement in the right direction, that movement creates inertia and inertia creates power. The power of that forward movement can lead them eventually to believe. It's the joining together of action and belief that gives us power. It doesn't matter which one comes first—they just have to eventually come together.

In business, it's important to remember this unusual relationship between belief and action. The business world is fast-paced and ever changing. There is always the need to be doing something to either gain advantage, not lose an advantage, or sometimes to just survive. Taking no action *is an action* and in business often times it can lead to losses in market share. If you're a decision maker and it becomes clear to you what needs to be done, don't let your internal belief that it might not work be what stands in your way. If you've done your due diligence and you're convinced the path is likely right, then take action. See if that action leads you to have belief as events unfold.

How do you know if belief and action should come together? You need to be paying attention. That's the next step.

Step Three: Consciously Monitor Your Thoughts and Actions

If you're going to pursue excellence you need to be constantly asking the question that every good ship's captain asks: *Where are we?* As I've mentioned already, vigilance is required in this process if you want to keep it on track. How can you pursue excellence, or anything else, for that matter, if you're not constantly checking your position and your progress against your map and your intended destination?

I try to be so thorough in this step that I even apply it all the way down to the level of penmanship. Frequently I can find myself needing to complete forms on behalf of a client. I sometimes look down and notice that my writing is getting sloppy. What if my assistant can't read this later? What if *I can't read this* later? When I find my penmanship slipping and not approaching excellence I'll tear up the form and start over. That wastes time and creates aggravation. On the other hand, if I don't do it right it can waste even more time, create more aggravation, and maybe cost me money and my client relationship down the road.

The monitoring process is critical in both your personal life and in business. If you let yourself hang on to a bad choice, or a choice that just isn't working, you will find yourself falling far short of excellence and rarely being in a position to win. Read this next line out loud and listen to how ridiculous it sounds: *Clearly I've made a bad choice and what I'm doing is an epic fail. I simply have to keep doing it no matter what. I don't have any good reason to think this, but I know it will get better.*

Nobody who reads those words out loud will think that this is the right attitude to have when undergoing self-examination or looking at your current business practices. Despite that, I also bet you know of situations where somebody did exactly that and I bet some of those situations even involve you!

Why does this happen? Well, we have words in our language because we needed to invent them to describe something. We needed a word for this kind of behavior and we came up with *stubborn.* People can be stubborn about doing things when they are not working because they confuse *stubborn* with *determined.* They're not the same. Determined is what you need to be when you know all you have to do is work harder. Stubborn is what you are when you don't want to work just a little bit harder to figure out what's wrong. Determined tears up the illegible application form and starts over. Stubborn finishes the form with even sloppier handwriting, throws it at their assistant, and then loses a client later when a mistake surfaces.

Self-monitoring is a simple function of mindset. Excellence is a mindset. Every day we need to be asking ourselves: How am I doing? Am I on track? Do I believe? Am I taking the right actions? This goes for a business unit as well as an individual. Measuring yourself against standards in pursuit of your company's goals is critical. It can't just be the dollars and cents, either. It also has to be the "sense" of where your people are and how your internal culture is responding. It's the tangibles and the intangibles.

When do you ever give yourself a break in this monitoring process? The answer is never! Pursuing excellence, being excellent as a human being, needs to be fundamental to who you are. You would never say, "I think I'm going to take a day off from breathing today. I'll just catch up on my breaths tomorrow." If you did try to do that, you would fail because breathing is autonomic; it happens whether you choose to do it or not. Pursuing excellence doesn't afford you that luxury. It's a choice. You need to make it and you need to constantly monitor your progress in the journey.

Step Four: Never Stop Practicing

I have a phrase I love to use that I think states this point so well I could just write it here and leave it at that (but I won't): polished practice leads to perfect performance.

This is where my experience as an athlete, not just at the professional level but from the very beginning, has perhaps had its greatest impact on me winning elsewhere in my life. I'm certain that you get rewarded in the light for what you have done in the dark. Everything the typical NFL fan knows about any particular football player is based upon a three-hour event they watch one per week during the fall. More to the point, because of the nature of the game of football, that fans come to know about that player through only a handful of plays, a few total minutes, during the course of that three-hour game.

There is so much more to that player's performance than those few minutes. Hundreds upon thousands of hours of practice behind the scenes that the fans never see. Even more hours are spent deeper behind the scenes that perhaps the player's coaches and teammates never see (like me dribbling out in the street late at night as a kid). That polished practice leads to that perfect performance.

Perfect? Desmond, nobody performs perfectly. Nothing is "perfect." It isn't attainable. Consider this: back in January 2006, a man who is in the nation's heart and mind as I write this, Kobe Bryant, had a game against Toronto where he scored 81 points. It was the second highest-scoring game in NBA history, behind Wilt Chamberlain's untouchable 100 points (as a fun aside, Chamberlain has twelve of the top twenty highest-scoring games of all time in the NBA—talk about excellence!).

Back to Kobe. In that 81-point game, he was 28-46 shooting and 7-13 from three-point range. He was also 18-20 from the free throw line. None of those numbers are technically perfect. Why then do most people who follow basketball refer to that night for Kobe as being "perfect?"

Because everybody knows that being literally "perfect" is something abstract. In the real world, we use the word perfect in a practical way that simply suggests *nobody realistically could do any better than that person just did.* That's the kind of perfect performance you're striving for when you engage in polished practice. In that sense, Kobe was perfect back in 2006.

Police units, firefighters, members of the US Armed Forces—all are constantly engaged in practicing. They train at academies and boot camps in order to start in their positions, but once they are in they are constantly practicing. They know that lives depend upon them doing their jobs in the most difficult of circumstances. Even if they knew what to do yesterday, they have to make sure they know what to do tomorrow. That means they can never stop polished practicing. Their job performance is a lot more important than Kobe's was that night in January.

Practicing isn't at all about how good you already are or how well you're currently doing. It's not about maintaining;

it's about advancing. When I was in high school on that very talented team I mentioned earlier, Coach Jones asked our team one day, "Do you know why we practice so hard when we are already so good?" His answer was that we wanted to be so good that when the game started, it was going to be easy for us compared to how we practiced. NFL players who played for the New England Patriots said the same thing about that team. The Patriots have been to nine Super Bowls and won six under Belichick and Brady because the practice so hard that the games are easy.

The Patriots are famous for having "experts" say they are not the most talented team. Yet they win all the time. Why? Because all that polished practice honed their skills. Talent is natural; skills are learned. Polished practice is a great teacher of skills.

Coach Jones likes to say that everything in sports and life is about preparation and practice. If you set a good foundation, put forth the effort, have the right attitude, you will win about 80 percent of the time. If you push yourself *really* hard then you can get that number to 90 percent. His coaching record over the years, and the success of the people outside of the gym who have played for him would suggest that he's onto something.

This need for practicing is in everything you do and it's a constant process. How you do some things is how you do all things. Don't ever let yourself start to say I need to practice here, but over there I'm already good enough. Remember the firefighters. Keep practicing. To become a champion, which means winning above all others, you need to practice harder and do even the little things better than the competition. When it comes to winning in life, the competition is you. You're always trying to take yourself to that next level.

Those are the four basic steps to pursuing excellence. I have a few more thoughts to share with you on things to look out for and other tips to keep you on the right path. Keep reading. I think they are excellent!

Keeping a Balance in All Things Excellent

I get asked a lot by people, "Desmond, how do I balance things in my life? How do I know I'm not sacrificing too much of one thing for the sake of another?" It's actually not just a fair question, but it's a really important one. Nobody wants to let themselves get so obsessed with one thing that they lose another due to neglect. I shared earlier how I won't sacrifice my time with my daughter for the sake of a business outing or client opportunity. That is a sort of balance being kept. I do think it's more complex than that so let me share my take.

Most commonly, when people talk about maintaining balance they are talking about things occupying a similar amount of space or time in your life. A very common model that most people have at least heard of conversationally is the mind-body-soul triangle. This triangle, when depicted, is always shown as an equilateral triangle (all sides the same length). This implies that every day you need to do something to challenge your mind (crossword?), body (planks?), and soul (watch Oprah?). Whatever you choose, you just have to keep that triangle in mind.

I see it a bit differently. I don't think that balance is about things being equal. I think balance is about not tipping over. Life doesn't allow us to get to the gym each day or read a passage from a book of meditations. In our pursuit of excellence, each day will have realities in it that dictate what we need to get done. We need to make sure that when we have to turn our attention and focus to one specific area for the time required to see a situation through, we don't neglect the other areas of life and our obligations to ourselves and others. Those areas may not get the attention at the moment that we would give them otherwise, but we won't let them fall into disrepair either. We'll get back to them just as soon as we can. Bottom line: when there is a shift in the load you're carrying, muscle up and carry it!

I also have a different model for areas of my life that I try to keep from tipping me over." As opposed to a triangle, I'm more of a fluid pentagon kind of guy. I have my Five Fs: faith, family, fitness, finance, and fun.

I am always trying to strike a balance in these five areas, and it's in each of these five areas that I set my own goals and standards of excellence. I'm constantly setting, chasing, checking, and practicing in each of these five areas. If I step back and just ask a basic question: *why am I practicing excellence*? It's to be the best I can possibly be in each of these Five Fs.

Be a Thermostat, Not a Thermometer

One problem people have in pursuing excellence is subjecting themselves to the outside influences and judgments of other people. It can be hard to stay on track when you run into friends or peers in your business who do not see eye to eye with you or your approach to life. While it's always right to be sensitive to what others are saying, it's even more important not to let yourself be controlled by it. That's where the thermometer and thermostat come into play.

A thermometer takes the temperature. It lets you know how hot or cold each individual room is, or each individual in that room (depending on the type of thermometer). Using a thermometer approach, you're always trying to adjust yourself to the particular temperature of the particular person or situation.

A thermostat, on the other hand, is used to set the temperature. You use it to make decisions on the climate you're going to create, and then you create the climate. It might be too warm for some and too cool for others. Some, however, are going to find it to be "just right." If you want to pursue your goals and be excellent you have to be a thermostat. Some may express they are uncomfortable and others may leave the room entirely, but you will be able to stay true to yourself and keep things at the temperature you want.

The rest of that metaphor is that you know full well that if you set the thermostat at 90 degrees you're going to drive just about everyone away. Factor in respect and common decency when setting your own personal thermostat.

Be Intentional and Careful with Who You Let In

While most people mean well, they don't necessarily understand your life and your story. They certainly can't truly understand your own personal journey towards excellence. We want to be open minded and we never want to shut out other people. That said, we also have to be careful about being unduly influenced by their advice. To use another great phrase from my father's recovery world:

take what you like and leave the rest behind. Be deliberate when choosing the people who influence you. Look for people who show a high emotional intelligence (EQ). These are the kinds of people who are best able to put themselves in your shoes. Nobody can really do that, but some are better than others.

You also need to know who to turn to situationally for particular or critical advice in your journey toward excellence. A friend of mine who is successful, self-actualized, and knows a lot of people found himself in need of advice on a very difficult decision a year or so ago. This friend rarely asks anyone for advice. In that instance, he told me that of all the many people he knew and respected, there was actually only one person he would even think of asking. He did ask him, the advice was given and taken, and the positive results from that are still being felt at this writing. Ask the right people for the right kind of help.

Manny always told me to be very careful about who I let into my head and my life. He would say we are a product of our environment and our friends and other people are part of that environment. Choose them wisely. Gary Rabine lives by the rule that the best minds are innovative minds. Those are the ones he wants around him and those are the ones he turns to when needed. Two different takes from two different and successful men. Both work. Both are intentional. Both are careful.

Business Leaders: Know Your People!

As a leader of a business you need to know your people in order for your business to become excellent. Not all of your people have the same definition of excellence that you do. You need to understand theirs in order to get them to embrace yours. You can only do this by having intentional conversations with them.

Don't try to project your standards for excellence onto them. Talk to them and find out: *What are their standards? How do they perceive excellence?* I'm not suggesting, nor is it possible, to tailor your business to every individual employee. That would be a disaster. I'm suggesting that to the extent you can incorporate your people's ideas of excellence into your company's idea you will be all the more successful. Don't surrender to them—include them.

My faith always guides me. 1 Corinthians 12:14 tells us, "the people that are the whole of humanity, are a team. The body is not supported by one person, but by all of us. We are one, we are strongest working together in unity. Teamwork is the key to living life in harmony, so that we can do God's will." I believe in that in our business and personal lives.

Don't Lie to Yourself and Don't Cut Corners

I like to tell people when bragging about my healthy diet and lifestyle that I'm "plant-based." The problem is the other night I had a couple of sliders at 2:00 a.m. I guess the better thing for me to say to people, and really to myself is, "I'm plant-based most of the time and occasionally treat myself to something just a little decadent." A little wordy, but truthful.

When you lie to others, you lose credibility. We all know that. What we don't stop to think about is that when we lie to ourselves we also lose credibility but with a more important audience: us. Be truthful in what you tell yourself about what you will and won't do on your journey to excellence. Remember the part about beliefs and actions? If you start on a path but are lying to yourself about what you will and won't do, you will make it hard for you to believe in you. Why would you? You're lying.

Same goes with cutting corners. We all know what happens when an architect does that. The house falls down. I never want to experience failure on my way to excellence and hear myself say, "Damn. I should have taken the time and done that better." Do it right. Do it thoroughly. Build a strong foundation.

Enjoy the Journey

Michael Jordan was arguably the greatest basketball player of all time (but that Wilt Chamberlain statistic is hard to ignore). He won six NBA championships and collected a trophy case full of individual awards. An extraordinary career, to be sure. But he didn't win the NBA title every year. He wasn't the NBA MVP every year. There were years along the way where he didn't win, but the entirety of his NBA journey was extraordinary. If he had waited for the end to enjoy it, he might have said he was disappointed with his whole career. He didn't win anything in his final season. Each and every moment along the way you need to take a pause to enjoy the journey.

I ask myself at the end of each day, "Desmond, did you do what you needed to do today to pursue excellence?" If I can answer yes, I let myself take the rest of the night off mentally. I savor it. It's like mowing a large lawn and then sitting on your porch with a refreshing beverage and enjoying the view. The grass is going to grow back. You're going to have to cut it again. But right now it looks just fine and you did it. Cheers!

Everything we've talked about thus far requires some really hard work. Hard work is, well, hard. How do you keep yourself motivated to get the work done along the path to winning? In the next chapter I'll share my tips and tips from others on how to be self-motivated.

Five Key Takeaways from This Chapter

- Define/create a standard of excellence for yourself.
- Choose your standards over your feelings.
- Practice with the focus of achieving mastery level of your craft.
- Continuously and Intentionally measure progress.
- Enjoy the wins, then get back to work.

CHAPTER 7

BEING SELF-MOTIVATED

> Good, better, best. Never let it rest. Till your good is better, and your better is best.
>
> —St. Jerome

During my first training camp with the Denver Broncos, a scout told me that I was "doing everything [I could] to not make this team." He could tell I was underperforming. I had no room to underperform as I sat fourth on the depth chart behind a future Hall of Famer (Shannon Sharp), a future All Pro (Byron Chamberlain), and a guy so big his nickname was House (Dwayne Carswell) and he, too, was a future All Pro. I was convinced I couldn't make the team.

I happened to be the *only* person who was convinced that I wasn't going to make the team. No coach said it. Nobody on ESPN said it. To be honest, nobody on ESPN was likely saying anything about me at all. I wasn't at a level where I was on the radar screen of Mel Kiper, Lee Corso, or anyone else that ESPN might have predicted a rookie's future.

No football expert had to tell me I couldn't make the team. I told myself. I knew I could run routes and catch passes extremely well, but the other guys had different skills that I simply didn't yet possess. I looked at them and decided I wasn't going to be able to take their spot on the roster.

The next thing that scout said to me has stuck with me to this day and may likely have been the reason I made it in the NFL and is almost certainly the reason I'm writing this chapter on self-motivation in this book.

He said, "You've got to stop comparing yourself to them. What you've got to figure out is how good *you* want to be. After that, you have to be honest with yourself and ask how good you are now. Then, set out each and every day with a focus to get better at one specific part of your game, every practice."

That was the key for me. I had to figure out what I wanted to be. My motivation couldn't come from those other tight ends around me. My motivation had to come from becoming the best tight end I could be for my own self and for my own sake. I had to want it for that reason, and that reason alone.

That word *want* was the key. That was what I had been missing. With the want I felt at that moment came the self-motivation I needed to practice harder; to push myself to my own limits not to the limits of any of the other tight ends. Suffice it to say that wanting worked. I made the roster and I eventually made it to a Super Bowl. I wish I could remember the name of the scout who scolded me that day. I owe a lot of my personal winning in life to him.

My only way to thank him is to pay it forward and share with you what I've learned about the important step of self-motivation on the path to winning.

In general, I don't think people consider the notion of self-motivation with the proper amount of seriousness or depth in their thought. Most people if asked will say, "Yeah, I'm self-motivated. I get the stuff done I have to. Nobody has to tell me to do anything." That isn't the kind of self-motivation I mean when I identify it as a key step on the path to winning in life. I'm talking about something deeper and I'm talking about a real focus on the word *self.*

Too often, people are taking their direction and receiving their motivation from the external world. They are focused on the other three tight ends in front of them on the depth chart and not on themselves. If I'm saying I'm self-motivated because I get stuff done that other people expect or tell me to do, then I'm being motivated by them, to act for them. While it's necessary in life to do the things that other people require (it helps you to not fail a class, get fired, or have your spouse put you on the couch), the kind of self-motivation I am focused on is the kind that makes you *want* to improve the *I* in yourself. It's independent from outside influences.

What I learned in that first training camp after the scout gave me my Rocky-Adrian moment, was that I wasn't competing against three other guys. I was competing against me. Having those other three tight ends around just added some additional fuel to the fire that the scout lit in me that day. I started to compete each day with myself yesterday. I needed to be better than him. If I was better than him, I would eventually be good enough to beat them, whoever they were.

A friend of mine tells the story of being in a difficult finance course in college. He had a very high GPA but was struggling in this class. He went to the professor, a tough old chain-smoking, horned-rimmed glasses type from Notre Dame, to try to get an idea of what would be on the exam so he could protect his precious GPA. The professor literally picked up a textbook and threw it at him. He shouted, "Quit worrying about your g@#$%&m grade and worry about learning the material. Your grade will take care of itself."

That lesson from the classroom is just as clear as the lesson I learned that day on the football field, and it's a lesson that needs to be learned by anyone who wants to win. He needed the self-motivation to master the material, to become as smart as he could be. If he could do that for himself, the external measure, the grade (making the roster) would follow.

So many of the decisions I made that slowed me down in life on my own journey toward winning were the result of doing things for, and because of, other people and their expectations. Once I learned that my motivation had to come from within me, and for me, I started to elevate my performance in everything in my life to a whole new level. That is what I want you to be able to do and be able to feel. I want you to be self-motivated so that the stuff you get done is your stuff, not just someone else's.

Hopefully, that opening gets you self-motivated enough to keep reading. If so, please read what comes next for you, not for me or anyone else.

You Need a Vision

Several years ago, when I first started running 5Ks, I would typically get up and run in the morning, or sometimes in the afternoon if my business day required an early start. For those who feel like the metric system is for our Canadian neighbors, five kilometers is equal to 3.1 miles. One night, before what would have been a typical run, I set a goal for myself: I wanted to break the twenty-six-minute mark, meaning to finish in under twenty-six minutes. That night, I took off motivated to win.

I lost. I came in at 26:11. I was twelve seconds off from where I needed to be—twelve seconds! If I had only pushed myself harder. I was angry. So angry, in fact, that the next morning I got up at 4:30 a.m. because I couldn't sleep. I got dressed and went for another 5K run.

This time I finished it in under twenty-six minutes. What I had done was just for me. Nobody knew (except for my wife who had to listen to me complain about it the entire night). My 5K run wasn't covered on ESPN 3 at 2:00 a.m. after a cheerleading competition. I knew. I won. *I wanted* it. I was motivated to get myself to my vision of coming in under twenty-six minutes. No praise or acknowledgment from anyone else could have topped what I felt for myself.

In the last chapter I talked about the chicken-and-egg problem of action and belief: which comes first? When I set my goal of running a 5K in under twenty-six minutes, I don't know if I really believed I could do it. That said, I had a vision and I was motivated to reach the goal. I took action. Once I came in only twelve seconds higher than I needed to be, I came to believe that I could achieve. The action led to belief which increased my self-motivation. Once belief kicks in, then self-motivation becomes almost automatic. It's easier to work toward something if you believe you can really do it. Sometimes you have to get started in order to start believing. It gives you a reason to believe.

One of my mentors, Gary Rabine, likes to say that for vision you need to have a picture in your mind of where you want to be ten years in the future. He thinks you should also set a vision for one year out and one month out. Those short-term and long-term sight lines are what work for him. Gary feels the need to compete every day because he always wants to win. Setting his vision keeps him focused on what winning means.

However you set your vision, whether in a timeline or just with simple goals, you need to get that vision set. If you don't, you won't be able to self-motivate. Self-motivate for what? It would be like an athlete getting all fired up and running out onto a field, and then stopping to ask, "Hey, what sport are we playing anyway?"

You Can Win One for the Gipper—but Not Every Time

Anybody who watches sports knows the scene where the star athlete comes out before the game and says, "I'm going to go out there today and win this one for my (fill in the blank)." In American culture, the most famous example of this is from the speech Knute Rockne gave to the Notre Dame football team at halftime of the 1928 Army game. Rockne telling the team about their former star George Gipp who had died a few years earlier, and who, while on his deathbed, had supposedly told Rockne to tell the team to "win one for the Gipper" someday if he felt they needed special inspiration.

If Notre Dame had not beaten the Cadets that day the story never would have become legend. Today, people routinely use that phrase and have no idea from where it actually came. The Notre Dame team got motivated to win for someone else, someone they had never even met.

There's nothing wrong with external motivation. There is no way to say it's bad to win one for the Gipper, for your mom, or for your newborn baby. Those special moments and sentiments can definitely help raise your level of performance. They're real and valuable, but they're not sustainable.

The only person who can be with you all the time is you. The fire for winning has to be lit inside of you. Some sort of external event or special person can temporarily fan that fire, but they can't light it. You have to do that. Even if you can barely get it to flicker, you still have to get it lit though self-motivation.

My high school football coach, Ernest Joe, remembers how we had a really big running back on our team who was a good friend of mine. He really was an amazing physical specimen and at 220 pounds he could really run over without even trying. The problem was, he wasn't running over people. He had lost his motivation.

One day at practice, I challenged him to go head to head with me in a hitting drill. I goaded him on a bit and you could tell I had him agitated. He was lot bigger than me and having a "little" guy challenge him got him fired up. We lined up in a three-point stance and went at each other full force. I hit him as hard as I could and he hit me just a bit harder. I injured my shoulder and missed a little time. As for my 220 friend? He woke up. He started running over people again.

Coach Joe gives me credit to this day for motivating that running back. I didn't, not permanently, at least. I just fanned the fire that was already in him. It was almost out, but it was lit. From that moment on he was self-motivated and he was successful. He was motivated for himself, not for me.

Every Tuesday I wear a pink shirt to honor my mom who fought a valiant battle against cancer. I think about her every day, but on Tuesday she is especially on my mind, at my lips, and in my heart. I feel her presence and it helps to especially motivate me to be all of the things I need to be on Tuesday. I'm winning for my mom, but if I didn't have it inside me to want to be the person I am, I would ultimately fail. I would have given this up a lot of Tuesdays ago. She fans the flame she helped me light years ago.

Internal and external motivation can be powerful when you're able to make them come together. Each week when I played football, we would have the external motivation of the opponent we were about to face, and we would have the internal motivation to make ourselves better individual players. If we could keep our focus and bring those two things together on Sunday, it would make us all the more difficult to defeat.

External motivation can be a supplement to, not a replacement for, the self-motivation required for winning. No one can *make you*—you have to *want to* and you have to make yourself. If you can give 100 percent of yourself, for yourself, to something, then you can win.

Beware of Rivalries: Remember Who the Real Opponent Is

There is no question that "rivalries," opponents against whom you have some sort of history that gets your attention, can sometimes help to motivate you. In a team sports situation, like the Bears-Packers game, you know that all the fans and the media are hyper-focused on the game and that it really matters to them. That can certainly help to get you focused on your preparation. That noted, rivalries and their impact on your motivation and performance are a little more complicated than you might think at first glance.

No matter what your situation, you always have to ask yourself why you want to "beat this team?" Why do you want to succeed? What is your vision in this case? The answers to these questions ultimately have to relate to something inside of you. That's why we call it self-motivation. If you lose track of that, you will lose track of your own performance.

One of the worst games I ever played was against the Seattle Seahawks in the playoffs. A playoff game is like a rivalry in that you have a different sort of atmosphere that is surrounding your regular workday. I was pumped up and trying to practice all week before that game in a way like I had never practiced before. All I could think about was beating the Seahawks. That was the problem. That was all I was thinking about. I got distracted from my regular discipline of being self-motivated to just keep improving my own performance as a football player *for me.*

Fortunately for me, the team won that game in spite of me. Afterwards, the coach came up to me and said, "Hey, whatever you were doing last week to prepare, don't do that anymore. Go back to your regular routine." My obsession with the external caused me to forget about the internal.

Over time I learned to treat the Bears-Packers game as just another game. They were just another opponent. That attitude made me perform better. My self-motivation was to be the best player I could possibly be, all the time. That meant that I needed to prepare to be my best against *every* opponent, not just the one four hours north.

Don't Lose Track of You by Focusing on Your Competition

This is a little bit like the rivalry warning, but it's especially focused on businesses and the workplace. We live in a capitalist country where everyone talks about competition. We're told that competition brings out the best in a company because it forces them to offer better products at lower prices. On a micro scale, we are told that workers in a company perform better when they are forced to compete against others in their department. This is a really common approach with sales leaders who deliberately try to pit their own salespeople against one another to drive their performance.

While it's kind of hard to stand against the status quo, and while as a professional athlete I certainly understand competition, I do want to give the warning that focusing too much on your competition can have a very bad side effect: It can make you too reactive instead of proactive.

I was told a story by someone who had the opportunity to speak at both Microsoft and Apple. Those two have a competition going on that rivals Coke versus Pepsi, maybe even Bears versus Packers. The gentleman told me that after the Microsoft presentation he took out an Apple smartphone and started discussing it with a Microsoft executive. The Microsoft executive became almost obsessed and he launched into a philosophical conversation about every feature and function of the phone.

Later, he had the occasion to be with an Apple executive. When he pulled out a Microsoft smartphone the response from an Apple executive was, "Oh, Microsoft has a very fine phone." That was it. Apple could not have been less interested in the Microsoft phone, while the response at MS to the Apple competitor was 180-degree opposite. Given that Apple has nearly one-half the market share of US smartphones, leaving all others to fight for the other half, their approach to worrying about themselves and not Microsoft might seem like a winning one.

I'm not suggesting that a company should ignore the competition. That would be foolish. You need to have awareness but you can't let that cross over into obsession. Every company has to work on making themselves and their product or service better. I'm not an economist, but I think there is something to the idea that a quality supply of something can create its own demand. There was no demand for a smartphone before Apple introduced one. How could there be? They didn't exist. They have maintained their market position over time by focusing on doing what they do best, not by focusing on what Microsoft is trying to do.

Bottom line is that if you suck (technical business term), what your competition is doing really doesn't matter. You don't want to place yourself in a reactive and defensive position. Your company needs to be self-motivated to produce the best product and service it possibly can and to improve that product and service every single year. Then and only then can you win in the marketplace.

The same thing holds true for each employee. If you're obsessed with the sales' numbers put up by your peers, then you will lose focus on developing the strategies and techniques you need to employ to sell more on your own. Do you think that Michael Jordan, Kobe Bryant, or Lebron James ever worried about their teammates while they were practicing? Do you think they worried about any other team? Worry about your own performance. Don't let a boss who never got little league coaching out of their system try to draw you into worrying about what the person in the next cubicle is doing. You're the one trying to win and you're only really competing against yourself.

Self-Motivation Requires Self-Awareness and Self-Control

Being self-motivated doesn't mean going crazy at everything you do in order to realize your vision. Winning in life is not about who is strongest in the moment (like it often is in sports), it's about who is strongest the longest. The who, of course, is you! You are your own competition. You want to see if you can outlast yourself through your entire lifetime.

As a competitor, you have to be able to see the big picture. Your life is, hopefully with God's grace, a long game. Having violent ups and downs, constant shifting of gears, can wear you out over time. You don't just need *constant* self-motivation; you need *consistent* self-motivation. As I mentioned before, it's about balance and not tipping over. Self-motivation can cause you to tip over if you lose control. My constant awareness of my Five Fs (faith, family, fitness, finance, and fun) are what I use to not just keep me motivated, but also to make sure that I keep all of them constantly and steadily moving forward.

The simple truth is that you can't always be moving up and down while at the same time enjoying sustained success. You need to learn to throttle yourself in a way that doesn't hold you back, but also doesn't let you careen off the path toward your vision.

Stay Self-Motivated for the Right Reasons

The process I'm outlining in this book is just that: a process. It's value-neutral. Anybody can use it for any purpose. This process could just as easily be used by a David Koresh as it could by a Mother Teresa. I'm trying to show you a way to win in life. What *you choose* to win is up to you.

That said, I don't think anyone is reading this book with the intention of learning how to be a more prolific Bernie Madoff or Jack the Ripper. I believe that if you're reading this, you're likely a good person who has experienced some success and is looking for ways to be better personally and/or professionally.

This self-motivation step is placed where it is in the process because if you've worked at the first three with intentionality and commitment to living a life rich with visions and values, you will be able to use the ideas from this chapter to help successfully pursue them. People can use anything good for bad and vice versa. I'm assuming that you want to use good for good so let me give a couple of tips.

If you took the first step seriously, you're going to want to protect your name and your word. Being self-motivated will help you to hold to the suggestion I made in that chapter for being consistent and reliable. Make keeping your name and your word intact one of the goals you're self-motivated.

Next, we talked about relationships. There is a lot of intentionality and hard work involved in creating, maintaining, and restoring relationships. You will only be able to pull that off if you're self-motivated to make certain you're doing the daily required work. If you rely on outside motivations to secure your relationships, you will find them not-so-mysteriously slipping away.

Finally, that commitment to excellence. There I talked about the need for vision, just like at the start of this chapter. The excellence "eye" and the self-motivation "eye" must have their vision aligned and in focus. Anything less will lead to dizziness, headaches, and total loss of direction and balance along your path to winning.

Everything about how you self-motivate is your own personal choice. Two different people can be confronted by the same situation of personal challenge or adversity and how they choose to handle it and move on from it can be completely different. It's my hope that you'll use the tool of self-motivation to make choices in your life that are positive, that are consistent with your vision and your values, and that those lead to winning for you and for those around you. Whatever the case turns out to be, it will be a byproduct of your own choice and your own effort.

Don't Dismiss the Realistic as Unrealistic Too Soon

When I met the woman who would become the most special lady in my world (not above, or instead of, my mom or daughters—moms and daughters are different), she shared with me that she had a dream of someday becoming a physician's assistant. I asked her what was stopping her? She pointed to the years of school required, the certifications, how she already had life obligations that were holding her back. In short, it just didn't seem to be a realistic vision for her to pursue.

I challenged her a bit. I said, "Why not take the first class and get started?" To her credit, she did. I'm not sure if she really believed she could pull it off when she started, but she took action. After those first few courses, she began to believe. Then I watched the transformation in her and I saw the self-motivation kick in. Suddenly, the unrealistic became realistic. Ultimately, she carried herself beyond the PA career path and now is on her way to becoming a pharmacist. Imagine, she is about to accomplish something today that yesterday wasn't just unrealistic, it was whatever comes after unrealistic!

Sometimes people just can't see the pathway to the vision that is barely visible to them through the fog of their own self-doubts and fears. We can sometimes help others clear their own sightlines and see the path. There were people that did that for me when I was young. People like both Coach Jones and Coach Ernest Joe. There were people who helped me do it when I was older, people like Coach Lovie Smith, and Mike Martz, and that scout whose name I can't recall. There have also been people post-football, like Gary Rabine and Manny Amezcua, who have made me realize that what seemed to be unrealistic wasn't unrealistic at all. I just couldn't see it clearly. One of the greatest services we can perform for others is to simply wipe the fog away and let them see what we see.

Having played pro football, there isn't really anything now that I want to accomplish that I think is unrealistic. If I'm able to think of it, I'm likely able to do it. Don't fret if you haven't played pro football. For anyone, there is a way to turn the unrealistic into the realistic. It isn't a magic trick and there isn't a shortcut.

The gap between a dream that may seem unrealistic and making it into a reality is one that can only be traversed by building a bridge. What's the bridge made out of? Hard work. No complicated engineering required, no sophisticated build of materials. Just intentional and focused hard work.

Sometimes when you're in the middle of that hard work, to bridge the gap between dreams and reality, you can start to look around and second-guess yourself. You can start to think, "Maybe this *isn't* realistic?" When that happens and when your motivation starts to lack, you have to ask yourself if there is any real evidence that what you're shooting for is unrealistic, or are you just making an excuse? It's easy to say, "I've always just been like this," but it's harder to ask yourself the next question, which is, "Do I have to be?"

Remember the rule of never lying to yourself. That means more than just being honest about what you aren't willing to do. It means not to lie to yourself about saying something isn't realistic, when you really just might be scared, inexperienced, or not willing to do the work to bridge that gap.

Sometimes what is realistic doesn't seem that way because it just isn't evident. The clearest example of this in my life was the possibility of playing pro football. All the time I was growing up, I never thought that was realistic, and yet, I ended up playing! It must have been realistic by definition! It certainly wasn't evident to me. I had people along the way, however, tell me they would help me see how to get it done. They were trying to show me the way. That's what we can always try to do to help others.

Turning the unrealistic into the realistic isn't really what we do when we go through this process. It was always realistic. We just couldn't see it. By starting with action, converting it into belief, putting in the necessary work, we can discover the realistic. A big key to self-motivation is to discover the realistic and to relentlessly move toward it.

Don't Trust Your "Feelings"

We're all human and that means we sometimes fail. How do we really know if we're failing? Sometimes we think we know because we get "feelings": anxiety, fear, or maybe just tiredness. While we may not be able to escape that as humans we are feeling animals, we do have to recognize that our feelings don't always send us the right signal.

The brain has a standard just like we have to set standards for winning. It keeps us on track. The brain's standard is to keep us out of danger. Unfortunately, since that part of our brain goes back to a time a bit more primitive than the twenty-first century, when it makes us feel like there is danger it isn't usually the kind that involves an impending storm or a saber-toothed tiger attack. These days, it's more likely it's the danger of inconvenience.

When you find yourself in a moment of self-doubt, when you're losing your motivation because you think something has become unrealistic, take time to consider your situation very carefully. Try to think rationally about why you might be feeling that way. What exactly are the feelings you're having? Are they based on something real? *Is* there something you can overcome? Are you misreading the situation?

We can feel pain and we can feel something is a great struggle. What you have to ask in each situation is: *is it worth it?* Don't lie to yourself. If it's not worth it, if it's not worth the feelings you're having, then it might be OK to stop. As long as that's a rational decision, and not an emotional one, it's OK. You just can't let your emotions get the best of you. If you're not going to be able to hit a goal and you decide it's not one that's worth hitting, step back and study it. Learn from it. Assess the situation rationally.

Don't let failure lead to yet another mischievous and harmful emotion: self-doubt.

Leaders: Encourage Self-Motivation!

By their very nature, most people don't like to be told what to do. They like to come up with their own ideas. Even if something isn't their idea, they sometimes need to at least *think* it is. As a leader, if you can let your employees generate their own ideas and create their own vision, at least to some extent, you'll find that their self-motivation will kick in. And there's no pay incentive you can offer that will make them outperform what they'll do if they're driven internally.

A business manager I know has overseen sales teams in different industries. One technique he always employs when generating a sales plan is to let each salesperson create part of their own plan using the kind of sales technique with which they feel they are most comfortable and most proficient. They have to be specific about what they're going to do, and they have to set measurable outcomes to be monitored, but part of their plan is to do what they want the way they want. They have to stay within acceptable company policy, but beyond that they are free to act.

The sales manager has found that across all industries and with all levels of salespeople, from top performers to the ones just getting by, everybody's level of performance increases under this method. He has found a way to make the people that work for him become self-motivated. As a result, they and the company start winning more often.

As I write this, I'm in the process of hiring new employees for my insurance agency. I'm asking them what is their vision for winning and how do they plan to incorporate this job into that plan? I want them to create their own expectations without me having to dictate to them. I also want to make sure they know that this job is not all I expect them to have going on in their life. I want this job to be one piece of a bigger puzzle for them. More about that in the next chapter.

Good leaders create voluntary and inspired followers. Nothing makes a person more inspired than being able to follow themselves while they follow you. Get your employees to share their vision and see how you can help to integrate with your vision for your company. Put the two together and watch the profits that come from a self-motivated workforce. You want your workforce to be like my friend and former teammate Byron Chamberlain describes when he says, "The perfect job is one that you would be willing to do for free, but you sure are glad they pay."

Self-motivation is all about that "want" I mentioned at the start of the chapter. If you can find the want, then you can achieve just about anything, even the things that you mistook for being unrealistic. The key is, once you achieve, don't stop. Set a loftier vision and set higher standards. Start over. If you can keep rising, your life will keep getting better and better. You won't just keep winning, your wins will get bigger. You'll cycle through self-motivation again and again. Ultimately, you may get to a point where you have to go to a dictionary to look up what "unrealistic" even means.

The "want" is what gives you the willingness for self-discipline and practice. A self-motivated person then experiences significant personal growth that leads to the entire cycle repeating itself. All that is left is to have an overriding passion and purpose for your life. That's what is needed to have a reason to actually win. That's the end game. That's the last step and I'll share it with you next.

Five Key Takeaways from This Chapter

- Self-motivation is about you and only you.
- The gap between a dream and reality is intentional and focused hard work.
- Don't trust your feelings—assess them.
- Focus on mastering the material; the winning outcome will follow.
- Leaders, integrate the visions of those you lead into the organization's vision.

CHAPTER 8

Having Passion and Purpose

> Find a job you enjoy doing, and you will never have to work a day in your life.
>
> —Mark Twain

I open with that quote because for all of the tips, advice, and experiences I'm about to share in the following pages really sums it all up. I know for myself and for the handful of other people I know who share this philosophy, none of us ever feel like we are getting up and going to work. We all feel like we are just getting up to continue on our life's journey. That said, please do keep reading because I'll have some other important points to share about having passion and purpose on your path to winning in life.

The two words—*passion* and *purpose*—for me are almost interchangeable. It isn't because I'm not aware that they don't have the same actual meaning. It's because for me you can't really have one without the other. I can't imagine the day coming where I say to a friend, "I really am passionate about everything in my life, but I don't have a single thing I want to do." The opposite is just as true. The reason I use both words is that in order to get the message through, it's helpful for some people to hear them both so that they can focus on bringing them together.

Life is difficult. The challenges we face every day as part of our daily routine can be great enough, but throw in the major ones and the unexpected ones and it gets even harder. Sometimes we need something to help pull us through the day. It's sort of like needing a helping hand even when there is nobody else around. Having passion and purpose in your life can give you that pull, that hand up, when you need it. It makes it easier to feel like you're not fighting *through* something, you're fighting *for* something.

The people I know in life who have passion and purpose are the ones that other people tend to see as go-getters. They seem to always have that little something extra to give. If you look around them, you won't be able to figure out how they do it. If you were able to look inside them, however, you would see their passion and purpose pulling them along.

Since my mom passed away from cancer a few years ago, I decided that a key part of my purpose in life was going to be to leave a legacy of helping my fellow human beings. I wear bright pink every Tuesday, in part, to make sure that I keep the passion alive for my fulfilling that purpose. While the dictionary definition of legacy points to leaving tangible things behind, I'm focused more on the intangibles I can leave by making a difference in people's lives.

Make Your Own Personal Statement of Purpose

When I got intentional about this, I came at it from the biggest of all pictures. After retiring from the NFL, I asked myself, "What does I want to do with the rest of my life?"

Since I was in my thirties at the time, I had a good number of years to go, so whatever answer I came up with was going to have to last. After a lot of soul searching and note taking, here is what I've made my own personal statement of purpose, about which I'm extremely passionate:

> With excellence being the standard, my purpose is to enhance the lives of others through any resource or expertise I may have available to me, within reason, and with respect to my family, who are my primary value. At every opportunity, I will transform associates and strangers alike into extended family members.

In terms of that last part, the part about transforming people into extended family members, just think how much I could accomplish, and help others accomplish, if I could build that kind of relationship with people all around the world? That part, and the rest of my purpose statement, helped to set the tempo for me for all of the great things that have happened since and that have led me to the point of where I'm now writing this book.

As I work through this chapter, you might find that this one is a bit more centered around me specifically than it is around general principles. That is in part because I share more clearly about developing passion and purpose if I draw from my own journey. It's also because I truly believe that to live your best life, the life that great minds have contemplated for centuries, you need the passion and purpose to help others. I want to give that gift to you.

What follows are my ideas that will hopefully help lead you to find your passion and purpose if it hasn't already become clear to you in life. Once you have it, and when you combine it with the previous four steps, nobody is going to be able to stop you from winning. Not even you!

Set Your Purpose with Purpose

It's common for people to ask the philosophical question, "What is my purpose in life?" I think that process is backwards. Asking yourself what your purpose is assumes that your purpose exists without you having any say in it.

Your purpose shouldn't be something you find; it should be something you define. Don't let your purpose in life be somehow chosen for you. Choose it yourself. As I shared already, I did a lot of soul searching and journaling on the path to defining my purpose. As my mentor and brother Manny Amezcua says, "The simple formula for happiness comes from having clarity in what you actually want, and what you are actually for, in your life." Notice he doesn't say anything about having fate or someone else make the choice for you.

Manny also taught me that in order to define your purpose you need to have enough self-awareness to understand where your passions and your gifts, or talents, align. Notice he doesn't mention skills. Skills are learned and the skills you choose to learn should, in part, be determined by what you need to fulfill your purpose. All of this makes good sense and seems almost obvious when you hear it or see it written in front of you. If it were so obvious, more people would be doing it successfully and nobody would read my book!

Manny is also the person who teaches that if your purpose statement isn't in writing then it isn't really a purpose. It's just an idea. Same goes for your plan to act in accordance with your purpose. That has to be in writing, too. Making the commitment to paper (on touch screen) is what starts to make a good idea into a great personal definition of purpose. Writing the plan can help make it realistic, something we covered in the last chapter.

When you commit your purpose statement to writing you have a way to track it and change it if you determine that is desirable or necessary.

My former Coach Alvin Jones believed in the need to be deliberate in creating your purpose. "Search your heart. You need a true reason for doing things. Raw talent can't overcome desire and work, and you can't work at something you haven't defined. Whatever talent God gave you will be squandered without purpose." Great advice from a man who helped to shape my life.

Every tombstone has one thing in common: the date the person was born and the date they died. But it's what's between those two dates that's important—the time in between is your life. You need to define what goes on between those dates. The first date is completely out of your control and the second date typically is. What goes in between, well, that is almost entirely within your control.

I've shared with you my personal statement of purpose, and I've shared with you the Five Fs that create my parameters. To show you how that can get even more thin-sliced when creating purpose, let me share with you how I used part of my general purpose and some of my key parameters to select a career.

Recall my five: family, faith, fitness, finance, and fun. During the time I made my living in professional sports, fitness was a key element. That was also before I got around to being intentional about developing a statement of personal purpose. Once I did that, I was out of football and in search of the right career.

Of my "five," I determined that "finance" was an area where I could not only take care of myself, but where I could help others take care of themselves and make a positive impact. I chose a career in financial services because that would allow me to make a living, while living my best life, and while helping others to do the same. I was intentional and I brought a sense of symmetry to my business life, personal purpose, and my personal need to pay the bills. Finance became the vehicle I used to help others in my day job. It became a purpose within my purpose and it was chosen intentionally, and in accordance with my own personal values.

The approach I took in choosing my career is one that you can take for creating any sort of "mini" purpose in your life. Find ways to stay true to your overall personal purpose and do things that are consistent with that and in support of it. That statement of personal purpose becomes your true north. Don't let it out of your sight.

For me, it's become an intrinsic part of who I am to want to serve others. While I can't force you to make service to others part of your winning purpose, I'm going to share a bit about the idea in the hope that the spirit of service will find a place in your passion and purpose.

Servant Leadership Has Made the Difference

My old football coach, Ernest Joe, moved from teacher to principal during his educational career. He made the move in part because he knew that by stepping into that role, he could serve the whole student body instead of just a few. He is an inspirational man by his very nature. He has incredible passion and energy, always shown through his upbeat manner and a contagious smile. He's also known for inspirational quotes.

Coach Joe says that when he took on the role, he made it clear to every student, and to every teacher, that he was working *for them*. He was going to do everything in his power to make each one of them successful. He wanted them to feel his passion and see that they were part of his purpose. He then began the process of day after day, school year after school year, walking the walk that went with his talk. He said that if he could demonstrate his service to them then everything about what he wanted to help instill in the students and the staff would become contagious.

While you may not have heard of Coach Joe prior to this book, I guarantee you that thousands who passed through his school know exactly who he is and the impact he had on their lives. That was his purpose in taking the job as principal and his passion in pursuing it was unquestionable. All the while he was the boss, he really was acting as a servant.

Gary Rabine takes the notion of servant leadership so seriously it has become the Rabine Companies' mission. Their simple statement, *Innovate to Serve*, is a direct reflection of Gary's own personal purpose. He says that he wants everyone in his company to come to work ready to serve their customers, fellow employees, and their community.

In my own case, I've evolved to the point of where that personal statement of purpose I shared is entirely about servant leadership. It's a higher calling. While I may have to develop "smaller" purposes for specific situations, no smaller purpose is ever allowed to contradict the larger one. That helps to keep me focused.

To some people, the word *servant* brings to mind the black-suited butler or the white-aproned chambermaid. You might ask, how can I be a servant to others without sacrificing my own opportunity to win? Good question. Keep reading.

Serving Others Doesn't Mean Not Serving Yourself

As you serve others, you might feel like you're emptying your cup every day. You can't possibly keep giving all you have. In fact, by definition you can only give all you have once. Once it's gone, it's gone. The workaround for that is to have others in your life who fill you up while you're filling someone else. That's why for me it's so important to build that community of others. It isn't easy, for me it isn't possible, to be in it alone.

I've said earlier in the book that I believe that going it alone is not a viable path to take if you want to win in life. While some might disagree, it's simply my perspective. Notice that everything I've written in this book has focused on your obligation to be responsible for your own actions and outcomes. I'm not contradicting myself by saying you need others. I'm saying that part of being responsible for yourself is to make sure you have built a support network around you to help you while you help yourself and others.

As far as the glass filling metaphor, I need people tapped into me while I'm tapped into others. I need to create a system flow. I find now that because of my own commitment to excellence and because of my level of self-motivation, I need roughly one person to help me replace what I use in helping ten people. That ratio is anecdotal, not scientific, but it seems about right in my world.

When I look back in my journals from 2012–13 I can see how I was writing frequently about my need to find the right kind of people to bring into my community to help me accomplish my purpose. It was in those writings that I came to realize that every person I reached out and helped ended up coming into my world and helping me. It was as if I had found a way to create a complete personal ecosystem that revolved around my passion and purpose. It fed it internally *and* it allowed for its expression externally.

Don't Let Yourself Go on Cruise Control

It's easy in our daily lives, a good deal of which can feel ordinary and repetitive, to let ourselves go on "cruise control," or "go through the motions," or "mail it in," or a host of other tired (literally) expressions. This is the hardest part of maintaining passion and purpose, and it's also the very reason you need passion and purpose. I think that might be called a paradox.

Every moment of your waking life ought to be intentional. They don't have to be, but if they aren't you're wasting those moments. Just because you're at rest doesn't mean you're unintentional. A state of rest ought to be for the purpose of recharging your own internal battery so you can be in a state of action later. You're not on cruise control when you're watching a little TV and enjoying an adult beverage at night. You're just at a light, waiting for it to turn back to green.

If you let yourself "cruise" too often, you'll find yourself neglecting, maybe even forgetting, your purpose. Without it, you can't win. What's the best way to avoid letting yourself coast and stop chasing your passion with purpose?

The answer creates the paradox. The best way to push yourself toward your passion and purpose is to actually have passion and purpose. Much like the case of how helping others causes them to help you help even more people. Having a passion and purpose is the best way to make sure you have the energy to keep your foot on the gas. It's hard to keep yourself pursuing something intentionally and all the time if you don't have anything to pursue. In fact, it's impossible.

If I look at my life, everything I ever relentlessly chased without letting up was something I decided was worth chasing in the first place. You can see the tight relationship between self-motivation and passion and purpose. Remember that this isn't science, it's a method that each person needs to adopt for themselves and make fit in the best way for them. You need all five steps. Just like going up the stairs, some people may take them one at a time, and some people might take a couple together.

Bottom line, when you stop to rest, leave your own personal engine in gear. When the light changes, go! Keep your foot on the gas at all times for control and acceleration. Self-driving cars are great—*for cars!* That's where the metaphor ends. You really are not a car. You're a thinking, feeling, and acting human being who has to keep going at all times under your own control and at the speed required. If you want to give up control, buy a Tesla. Maybe that will satisfy the urge.

Don't Try Too Hard to Control Passion

Passion is an emotion and we all know that emotions can let us lose our rationality. Being too emotional can lead to bad decisions in life and in business. We need a clear mind if we want to make good choices.

When I say that we don't want to control passion, any extremist could take that too far and try to point out what a mistake I'm making. Remember, however, at the start of this chapter I pointed to how passion and purpose come together for me as two unified parts of a single whole. Having my purpose and not losing track means that my passion can't get out of control. It might drive me harder at times, but since it's tied and unified with purpose, it just means it might get me there a little bit quicker.

My "Pink Tuesday" project for my mom is a good example. After she passed and I became committed to finding something to do that would extend her legacy and help others who were having their lives taken off a winning course by cancer, I started to look for a way to channel the energy. I turned to the American Cancer Society (ACS).

I learned about the ACS's Road to Recovery program. The program is a curbside-to-curbside transportation service that provides free rides to cancer patients to and from their cancer-related treatments. Trained volunteer drivers donate their time and the use of their personal vehicles to help patients get to the treatments they need. Public transportation vouchers and paid Lyft and Uber rides are other ways those who don't have means, or can't afford transportation to and from, are supported. That was something about which I could become passionate. The program helps real people in need in real time, with immediate, visible results. I was in.

I've become increasingly passionate about the program. Whether it's fundraisers I stage or events I attend, my passion for this program has driven me to do things I never would have imagined I'd have the time to do, or do even if I knew I'd have the time. I know that this uncontrolled passion has caused me to sometimes sacrifice other things. That's OK with me. I haven't lost my balance. I haven't tipped over. The program fits with my overall personal purpose statement and it fits with my Five Fs. Road to Recovery has me passionate and purposeful. It doesn't make me crazy!

How do you stop the crazy from kicking in? The best advice I have is to stay in your lane. That's another way of saying don't lose focus. When I started with ACS, I saw all of the different ways I could possibly contribute my time and energy to fighting cancer. My status as a semi-celebrity and the multitude of people I know would let me jump into all kinds of areas within ACS and do some amount of good. Doing that could also cause me to tip over.

I decided to make a choice, and that choice was Road to Recovery. Everything I do in this area is in that program. That sort of focus helps me to identify a clear purpose and tie it to my passion. Like a fast-moving rotational ride at the carnival, they can spin me around and make me feel the centrifugal force, but I'm tied in. I don't fly out of my seat.

One of the things I have learned from my father is that some people who suffer from addiction (not the kind where there is a physiological or chemical reaction—that's different) actually have an addictive personality where they can get addicted to anything from alcohol, to gambling, to Facebook, or anything else they start to spend too much time with as an escape or other outlet. If you have that kind of personality type, you do have realize that you can become addicted to your passion and purpose.

Sometimes turning to others is a good way to check your own behavior. Never be afraid to ask the people closest to you, "Am I OK? Do I seem at all out of control to you?" If you think you have an addictive personality, always be mindful of that first step in a different program and make sure your life isn't becoming unmanageable.

Don't Get Complacent—Don't Stop Paying Attention

Not letting yourself become complacent is the key to not losing your passion and purpose. The easy self-check for complacency is to take stock at the end of each day and ask yourself, "Was I thinking about my passion and purpose today? Did I win the day?" Just the discipline of having this process will make it more likely you will stay on track. We all know how setting an alarm at night can help cause us to wake up before that alarm in the morning. It's imprinted on our brain.

It's also important to continuously reevaluate where we are in our lives and how our current situation fits with our passion and purpose. We evolve. We change. I'm not the same person today that I was at age twenty-two, getting ready to leave college and head into the NFL. As we evolve our passion and purpose will evolve, as well. This is something we should embrace enthusiastically. It should be fun to have to reexamine where we are in life and how we might want to change where we are heading as a result.

I'm not suggesting we should change our core beliefs like we change our socks. If we did that we wouldn't be able to call them core beliefs. I'm saying that the focus of our passion and purpose might change as we change by learning more and growing as a person.

Let me share a very precise sort of example. When my mother passed away from cancer, I got myself wound up on having the purpose to do everything I could to attack that deadly disease. I started by being focused on wanting to raise money for any kind of cancer research known to man. If there was any cancer-fighting cause, then it could easily fit with my purpose. Then something happened. I started to get "educated" about the world of cancer. I was about to experience a change that would cause me to reexamine my purpose.

I began to get an exposure to the world of big pharma, the medical industrial complex, and all of the money that surrounds the cancer industry. In a way that almost makes me sad, I became a bit skeptical about our real desire to actually find a cure for all cancers. I came to feel that raising money just to throw into the cancer "machine" perhaps wasn't the best way to help people. That's when I adjusted my purpose.

I became passionate about, and dedicated to, the Road to Recovery program *b*ecause I knew that no matter what the cancer industry was all about, no matter what was really going on, this was a way to help real people right now. I changed my purpose because I recognized that I had changed.

That very significant change in me took place over a relatively short time period in terms of a normal lifetime. That means there is no set number of years or even days that you need to wait before reexamining who you are and how it fits with your purpose. You reexamine continuously. If you don't let yourself get complacent, this is easier to remember to do. As I wrote before, we keep what we have only with vigilance. The same goes for changing it!

Bottom line, if your purpose and passion do not align with what you believe then you will fail. You will constantly be fighting within yourself instead of fighting to win in life.

This idea of personal change and growth, coupled with reevaluating your passion and purpose, comes into play with personal relationships, as well. We all have either been in, or know someone who has been in, a relationship where we say, "I just don't feel the passion anymore." Make no mistake, I'm *not* a marriage counselor! What I know is that when things have truly changed within a relationship, and when two people might not believe that they can continue to be part of each other's purpose, whatever happens next from that point can't involve *giving up the passion to have that kind of relationship*. This one may not work, but you can't give up on making sure that you find one that does work.

We only get a chance to go at this thing called life once (at least with the consciousness that we have in this one). We can't allow ourselves to settle. I don't want to find myself at age ninety-five, almost out of time, and saying to myself, "I wish I hadn't settled for…" No time for do-overs. No free kick. No tenth chance. Tennyson had it right when he wrote, "Better to have loved and lost than never to have loved at all." Keep loving, keep losing, keep chasing the relationship part of your life with passion and purpose. When you hit ninety-five, you'll be very glad you did.

By the way, when you get it right, continue working through the five steps of winning to keep it right. Don't let yourself lose it because you got complacent!

Passion in the Workplace Is Not About Passion for the Workplace

Everyone who ever had a job that wasn't their dream job (most of us) knows the feeling of having to get up and go to work without feeling enthusiasm or energy for the day ahead. It can be difficult to have a sense of passion and purpose for a job that doesn't fit with what you feel you want in life. I have a friend who would have told you when he was a senior in college that the last three things he wanted once he graduated were to work *in* banking, work *for* the government, and live in New England. You guessed it: less than a year after graduation, he was doing all three!

The late and very wise Maya Angelou had a simple expression that addresses this problem pretty well. She said, "If you don't like something, change it. If you can't change it, change your attitude." My friend ultimately changed his work situation—fifteen years later! In the meantime, he didn't do a very good job of changing his attitude. The result was a lot of wasted years he can never get back.

Let's get basic. You don't *have to* go to work. Slavery was eliminated a long time ago in this country. Where you work, what you do, is still a choice. You might feel like your choices are limited at the moment, but it's still a choice. You could just skip work and stay home. The problem with that approach is that you just might end up homeless if you do. If you have to go to work just so you won't be homeless, and you can't change that fact at the moment, change your attitude.

One of the hardest things for us to do as people is to find and hold onto gratitude. Gratitude is something about which my father's recovery program is constantly teaching and reminding members. The first key to dealing with a job that is not the "one of your dreams," is to be grateful you have that job in the first place. We spend so much time today complaining about the things that aren't perfect in America, we forget to be grateful for the good things we have. This is a country where almost anyone who wants to find work can find work—maybe not the work they want, but work nonetheless.

The fact that not everyone has their dream job makes it all the more important for everyone to have an overriding passion and purpose for their life. It would be extremely unlikely that the job you have, even if it's your dream job, would be providing 100 percent of what you need to fulfill your passion and purpose if you had taken the time to decide what it was and start to move toward it. Your job might provide 80 percent of it or it might provide 10 percent of it, but it won't provide all of it. That's why you need to use that job you have to help you win in your bigger life that includes your work, but that isn't just your work. There needs to be more to you than that.

My same friend told me that when he finally had a chance to get out of banking, he wasn't sure he could be successful. He reached out to a friend who was very successful and asked him for advice. He said, "I've always been a banker. Can I be anything besides that?"

His friend changed his life with his answer. He said, "Dude, you're confusing what you *do* with who you *are.* You just *do* banking during the day. That isn't who you *are* as a person. You're much bigger than that." That encouragement was what he needed. Now he lives his life filled with passion and purpose and uses his work to help fulfill his own greater personal mission.

While you may not be able to fully experience passion and purpose in your work, you should be able to find a way to experience some. Look for that opportunity. Remember, it's your passion and purpose that help pull you through life. Finding some in your work can help pull you through your workday. Then you can go home, be grateful you have a home, and work on the bigger pieces of your life that matter.

That job you might not love, and the title you may not care about, might just what you need to give you the ability and credibility you need to make a difference and get you where you want to be. If you don't think that is the case, and you have the ability to make a change that works better for you, then change. Otherwise, change your attitude and get to work!

If You're the Boss, Find Your People's Passion and Purpose

I mentioned that right now I'm in the process of hiring people for my company. One of the questions I'm asking as I interview (a question most bosses would never ask) is, "How do you see using this job to help fulfill your own personal passion and purpose?" If you want to see an interviewee have to think on their feet, just ask them this question. They were not taught to prepare for this one in a LinkedIn seminar.

I ask them because I want them to think about working with and for me as part of something bigger that actually fits into their greater scheme of life. If it doesn't, there's a good chance they will come to see working with Desmond as just another "dead end" job. That won't serve them, the company, or me very well.

I also ask them because I want to know if I can do things to help them channel their passion and reach their purpose. Remember my own personal statement of purpose from the start of the chapter. I'm not just trying to hire someone; I'm trying to make a permanent impact on that person's life.

Just in case you don't really buy into the personal notion of making your employees' life a better place as being part of your obligation, then consider this: If showing interest in them makes them more passionate about your company's purpose, then they are going to be a more self-motivated employee. That improves top lines, bottom lines, and everything in between the lines.

Passion and purpose comprise the final step in the process that I've been privileged and humbled to be able to share with you. These five steps have been the secret to all the great things I've enjoyed, and continue to enjoy, in my life each and every day. I've been blessed by many people trying to shine light for me along the way so I could see those steps. I also spent time stumbling around in my own self-imposed darkness trying to discover them myself.

Hopefully, this book will help shine a little light for you so the path can be clear and the steps can be sturdy. I encourage you to walk along with me and never stop walking. The process is endless. It's a dream that for some, this book and these five steps may even help you to avoid having to walk the twelve steps that my father has been forced to have to walk in his life. As I shared in the beginning, it's his journey toward the twelve steps that played such a key role in having me discover these five.

May God bless you, inspire you, and strengthen you in everything you do. Time to close the book and start winning!

Five Key Takeaways from This Chapter

- Keep your hand on the wheel and your foot on the gas—don't go into cruise control.
- Passion and purpose aren't a search—they're a choice.
- Change "it" or change your attitude about "it."
- Passion and purpose will evolve over time—embrace it.
- Make a difference!

BEFORE YOU GO

It was such an honor to spend time with you throughout your reading of this book. I'd like to take just a few more minutes to make a request. It's not a large one.

If you enjoyed this book, would you be so kind as to take a moment, go to Amazon, and look up the title, "Principles of Winning," and leave a short review? Even if you only had time to go through a couple of chapters you will be able to leave a review and, if you desire, go back later and add to it once you've had a chance to complete the book. Your first impressions are very useful so don't worry if you have only time now to review one or two chapters.

Finally, note that books succeed by the kind, generous time readers take to leave honest reviews. This is how other readers learn about books that are most beneficial for them to buy. To this end, I thank you in advance for this very kind gesture of appreciation. It means the world to me.

ACKNOWLEDGMENTS

Grateful is the first word that comes to mind when I reflect on life. We encounter so many forks in the road, ups and downs, the thrill of victory and, of course, the agony of defeat. This is what makes life so great: the journey!

In my life, I've learned how to embrace the trials and appreciate the wins. Trust me, I've had my fair share of both. My ability to understand that this is what life brings and to evolve enough as a human to take life as it comes stems primarily from my faith in God. But if it wasn't for the people who were there to help me find my way through the trials, or those who enjoyed the sweet taste of victory with me (some are the same individuals), this journey wouldn't be as meaningful.

I could write ten more books about everyone who has played a significant role in my life thus far. For the purpose of *Principles of Winning,* I'd like to acknowledge those who contributed to the writing my second book.

First, I must thank the two people who brought me into this world: Rena Davis and Paul Clark, Sr. Simply put, without them there is no story. I like to say I learned what to do, and how to do it, from my mom. Although she's no longer here in the physical world, the example she set for us still carries on. Early in life I learned what not to do from my dad, until he changed his life and committed to being the great father he is today. Now he sets the example.

Maria Clark, you came into my life nine years ago and challenged me to be a better version of myself. We've gone through the highest highs and lowest lows together. Through it all our love for one another still prevails. It hasn't been perfect, but in the imperfection there are moments of perfect beauty that are as beautiful as you are. I wouldn't change it, ever.

I wish everyone could share the love I have for my brothers. Am I my brothers' keeper? Yes, I am. Ralph, Paul, and Dominique are my best friends. Thanks to all three of them for being themselves and for being great brothers. Let's keep making "her" proud.

Without the great coaches I had in my life, I promise you I wouldn't be here. Coach Jones and Coach Joe were father figures for me when I needed them. They both instilled solid principles in me that I continue to win with today.

My teammate Byron Chamberlain and that tight end room from 1999 set the tempo for my entire NFL career. The bar was set high from the very beginning and I did my best to keep it raised.

When I was writing in my journal back in 2012–13, searching for mentors I could continue to learn from and grow with in my new professional life, I didn't know that I would find the men I was looking for in Manny Amezcua and Gary Rabine. I couldn't have asked for better mentors and brothers than these two extraordinary people.

Last but not least, there's Brent Hamachek, who helped me get these thoughts out of my head and coordinate them in a way that is meaningful, thoughtful, and powerful. We are an odd couple but through this journey we found out we are brothers from another mother.

There are a few hundred other people I could thank as well—I'm grateful to these individuals not only for contributing to my life, but also for taking time to contribute to the book you're holding in your hands.

Made in the USA
Columbia, SC
16 April 2022

58982123R00100